HUGUE~~~

and

SCOTS LINKS
1575–1775

by
David Dobson

CLEARFIELD

Printed for
Clearfield Company by
Genealogical Publishing Co.
Baltimore, Maryland
2005

Reprinted for
Clearfield Company by
Genealogical Publishing Co.
Baltimore, Maryland
2008

ISBN-13: 978-0-8063-5284-8
ISBN-10: 0-8063-5284-1

Made in the United States of America

INTRODUCTION

The first Calvinist community in France was established at Meaux in 1545, and since 1560 the term Huguenot has been applied to French Protestants. Persecution of Protestants began after the Edict of Chateaubriant in 1551. The Colloquy of Poissy in 1561 failed to achieve religious agreement between the Catholic and Calvinist leaders of France. The Calvinist party was led by the Prince of Conde and Gaspard de Coligny, Admiral of France. Civil war in France then occurred between the Catholics and the Protestants which ended with the Peace of St. Germains, in 1570. Under this treaty the Protestant minority was allowed a degree of toleration. This, however, ended with the Massacre of St. Bartholemew's Day in 1572, which continued for about a week, ending with 3,000 Protestants having been murdered in Paris and a further 7,000 being killed elsewhere in France. Their leader had been Henry of Navarre; but when he ascended the throne in 1584, he converted to Catholicism. In order to provide the Protestant minority with some security in France, King Henry passed the Edict of Nantes in 1598. The Edict of Nantes guaranteed the Huguenots freedom of worship and integration into the social and economic life of France. Henry's successor, Louis XIII, was not favourably disposed towards the French Protestants and began to dismantle their defenses and rights. Huguenot military and political power was gradually destroyed and ended with the fall of La Rochelle in 1628. The French wars of religion officially ended with the Peace of Ales in 1629. Thereafter the French Protestants gave their support to the state and helped defend France from the threats from the Hapsburgs. As a consequence, King Louis XIV promised to uphold the remaining rights of the Huguenots, but these rights were again threatened between 1661 and 1679; for example, 570 churches were destroyed. On 22 October 1685 the "perpetual and irrevocable" Edict of Nantes was revoked. Thereafter all Protestant services were banned, all their churches destroyed, Protestant baptism was forbidden, but the Huguenots were forbidden to leave France. The outcome was that approaching a quarter of a million Calvinists fled from France to the Protestants countries of northern Europe, specifically The Netherlands, Germany, Scandinavia, the British Isles, as well as to America and the Cape of Good Hope.

Scotland officially became a Protestant country in 1560; and with the Presbyterians in the majority, it was a likely destination in which the French Calvinists could take refuge. There had been a small trickle of refugees and emigrants from France settling in Scotland, especially in Edinburgh, during the late sixteenth and early seventeenth century, but the main influx occurred in the last quarter of the seventeenth century. These people had advanced technological skills and had entrepreneurial talents which were much in demand in contemporary Scotland. Most of these emigrants—the craftsmen, artisans and merchants—settled in the Canongate, then a separate burgh but now part of Edinburgh. A number of French immigrants were employed as servants to the nobility and settled on country estates. The other main occupational group was those Huguenot refugees who joined Scottish regiments and fought against the armies of France or its Jacobite allies in Scotland and Ireland. The records of the French Protestant Church in Edinburgh do not seem to have survived, but a number of French Protestants seemed to have joined the Church of Scotland, another Calvinist church. The baptismal and marriage records of the churches in the vicinity of Edinburgh contain the names of French families during the seventeenth and eighteenth centuries. Such names also appear in the civic records. In order to achieve economic and social success in a Scots burgh of the time, it was necessary to become a burgess. One method to achieve that was by having served an apprenticeship under an existing burgess. The registers of apprentices and those of the burgesses contain the names of several French Protestants. The other main source of reference on the relatively elusive Huguenots was the burial register of Greyfriars churchyard in Edinburgh.

This book has been complied from both primary and secondary sources in Scotland and is based to some extent on distinctive French surnames, some which have become Scotticized and may vary from the original; for example Dieppe and its variants. In England some French surnames were translated into English equivalents, and this may also have occurred in Scotland, making it more difficult to identify Huguenot families.

David Dobson
St Andrews, Scotland, 2005.

REFERENCES

ABL = Aberdeen Burgh Letters
ABR = Aberdeen Burgess Roll
AMW= Accounts of the Master of Works, Volume ii, 1616-1649
BRC = Baptism Register, Canongate
BRCa= Baptism Register, Carrington
BRE = Baptism Register, Edinburgh
BRM = Baptism Register, Musselburgh
BRNL= Baptism Register, North Leith
BRSL= Baptism Register, South Leith
CBR = Canongate Burgess Roll
DAL = English Army Lists, C. Dalton, London, 1960
EBR = Edinburgh Burgh Records
EBR = Edinburgh Burgess Roll
ECA = Edinburgh City Archives
EPT = Edinburgh Poll Tax
ERA   Edinburgh Register of Apprentices
GED = A Directory of Edinburgh in 1752, J. Gilhooley,
       [Edinburgh, 1988]
GBR = Greyfriars Burial register
MRC = Marriage Register, Canongate
MRE = Marriage Register, Edinburgh
MRL = Marriage Register, Liberton
MRM= Marriage Register, Musselburgh
MRNL= Marriage Register, North Leith
MRSL= Marriage Register, South Leith
MRStC   Marriage Register, St Cuthbert's
PHS = Proceedings of the Huguenot Society of Great Britain and
       Ireland
PS = Painters in Scotland, 1301-1700, [Edinburgh, 1978]
RPCS= Register of the Privy Council of Scotland

HUGUENOT AND SCOTS LINKS, 1575-1775

AETHOW, THOMAS, a skinner, was admitted as a burgess of
Edinburgh by right of his father John Aethow a perfumer
burgess, on 13 July 1715. [EBR]

AGATE, STEPHEN, a French jeweller and goldsmith, was
admitted as a burgess of Old Aberdeen on 17 October 1696.
[OABR]

AINGER, EDWARD, regimental surgeon of the Dragoons, 1688.
[RPCS. XIII.li]

ALLEIR, FRANCIS, a comfit-maker, admitted as a burgess and
guilds-brother of Edinburgh by right of his wife Esther,
daughter of James Wallace a vintner burgess, on 18 December
1661. [EBR]

ANRAGNO, ANTOINE, married Helen Smith, in Duddingstone on
16 May 1611. [CMR]

ANTONIUS, DAVID, a mariner, whose testament was confirmed
on 8 September 1753 with the Commissary of Edinburgh.
[NAS]

ANTONIUS, HENRY, married Margaret Harper, at
Holyroodhouse, Edinburgh, on 30 March 1665. [MRE]

ANTONIUS, HENRY, son of the late Henry Antonius His
Majesty's kettle-drummer, was apprenticed to William Clerk
a wright in Edinburgh on 17 April 1689, [ERA]; a wright in
Edinburgh, married Esther, daughter of late James Vaus a
tailor burgess, in Canongate on 31 July 1696. [CMR]; and was
admitted as a burgess of the Canongate by right of his wife
Esther Vaus the daughter of a burgess, on 18 June 1698;
whose testament was confirmed on 14 May 1750 with the
Commissary of Edinburgh. [NAS][CBR]

ANTONIUS, JOHN, a wright, was admitted as a burgess of
Edinburgh by right of his father Henry Antonius a wright
burgess, on 29 March 1723. [EBR]; a wright in Monteith's
Close, Edinburgh, 1752. [GED.4]

ANTONIUS, ROBERT, a wright, was admitted as a burgess of Edinburgh by right of his father Henry Antonius a wright burgess, on 9 December 1720. [EBR]

ANTONNIASA, HENRY, was admitted as a burgess of the Canongate by right of his wife Esther Vass daughter of a burgess, on 18 June 1698. [CBR]

AQUTTER, RALPH, a musical instrument maker in South Kirk parish, married Elizabeth, daughter of William Hogg an advocate, in Edinburgh on 5 April 1709. [MRE]

ARAGO, DOMINIQUE FRANCOIS, secretary of the Academy of Sciences of France, was admitted as a burgess and guilds-brother of Edinburgh on 9 September 1834. [EBR]

ARMIGER, JEREMIAH, a merchant in London, around 1707. [NAS.RD3.114.354]

ARNEICE, CORNELIUS, a say weaver in Edinburgh 1750. [EBR.MB#vii.209/7559]

ARNOUS, PIERRE, a teacher of French, settled in Edinburgh 1779. [ECA.Aliens Register]

ATAMONG, JAMES, an instrument maker from France, who was admitted as a burgess of Edinburgh on 22 May 1674. [EBR, 22.5.1674]

ATTIMON, MARGARET, daughter of James Attimon a gunsmith burgess of Edinburgh, married Robert, son of Francis Henderson a gunsmith burgess, in Canongate on 14 July 1692. [MRC]

AUREGIUS, ANTION, married Helen Smyth, in the Canongate on 16 May 1611. [MRC]

AWIN,......, a surgeon from Paris, who was working illegally in Edinburgh around 1595. [EBR: 1.8.1595]

BABA, JOHN, a cordiner, admitted as a burgess of Glasgow on 22 January 1584. [GBR]

BABA, MICHAEL, a cordiner, was admitted as a burgess of Glasgow as son of John Baba, cordiner, 18 April 1616. [GBR]

BABY, PETER, married Elizabeth Smyth, in the Canongate on 26 March 1799. [MRC]

BACQUEWIKS, TIMOTHIE, servant of the Duke of Lauderdale, was admitted as a burgess and guilds-brother of Edinburgh on 26 September 1677. [EBR]

BAISLANS, NICOLAS, a gentleman, was admitted as a burgess and guilds-brother of Edinburgh on 17 August 1711. [EBR]

BAJINER, JAMES, a merchant, was admitted as a burgess and guilds-brother of Edinburgh on 30 December 1691. [EBR]

BALLFORT, PIERRE, a member of the French church in Edinburgh in 1713. [ECA.EBR,17.4.1713]

BANASTRE, GEORGE, Captain of Morrison's Regiment of Foot, was admitted as a burgess and guilds-brother of Glasgow on 30 March 1716. [GBR]

BANKEIR, GEORGE, a weaver, was admitted as a burgess and guilds-brother of Glasgow on 6 September 1732, being the eldest son of John Bankeir a maltman burgess and guilds-brother. [GBR]

BANKEIR, MALCOLM, a merchant, was admitted as a burgess and guilds-brother of Glasgow on 11 May 1655. [GBR]

BANKIER, MARGARET, married Hugh Gilmure, in Edinburgh on 22 April 1720. [MRE]

BAPTISTASETT, JOHN, master of the Lottery of the Royal Oak, permitted to advertise a lottery in Edinburgh, in 1664. [ECA.EBR:11.5.1664]

BARGARD, Colonel ALBERT, was admitted as a burgess and guilds-brother of Edinburgh on 24 February 1716. [EBR]

BARIN, DAVID, a silk weaver, was admitted as a burgess of the Canongate on 11 September 1704. [CBR]

BARNABIE, SUSANNA, married James Scot a practitioner of medicine in Edinburgh on 25 April 1703. [MRE]

BARNARDEN, GASTON, a Lieutenant of Marines, was admitted as a burgess and guilds-brother of Edinburgh on 10 April 1745. [EBR]

BARRANGE, JANE, married James Keir, in Edinburgh on 30 October 1748. [MRE]

BARRENGER, ROBERT, post-master, Barrenger's Close, High Street, Edinburgh, was admitted as a burgess and guilds-brother of Edinburgh on 10 May 1654, [EBR]; sergeant at arms to the Justice Court in Edinburgh was admitted as a burgess of Old Aberdeen on 1 October 1655, and as a burgess and guilds-brother of Glasgow on 3 May 1656. [OABR][GBR]

BARRENGER, ROBERT, a weaver in South Kirk parish, Edinburgh, married Jane, daughter of William Thorburn a mason in Dalkeith, in Edinburgh on 13 November 1748. [MRE]

BART, GEORGE, a Flemish cloth-worker in Edinburgh, 1614. [ECA.EBR.MB#vii.209/7559, 7561, 7568]

BARTHILMO, JOHN, a dyer, was admitted as a burgess of the Canongate on 21 July 1631. [CBR]

BASSE, NICOLAUS, married Christian Hunter, in South Leith on 17 September 1659. [MRSL]

BAYONET, BETHIA, married David Pedie a journeyman shoemaker, in Edinburgh on 20 March 1748. [MRE]

BEAUCHAMPS, Mrs MARY, late servant to the Marchioness of Douglas, whose testament was confirmed on 26 June 1718 with the Commissary of Edinburgh. [NAS]

BEAUCLERK, GEORGE, Major General and Commander of H.M. Forces in North Britain, was admitted as a burgess and guilds-brother of Edinburgh on 10 December 1756. [EBR]

BEAUMONT, JOHN, in Clapham, Surrey, whose testament was confirmed on 29 October 1739 with the Commissary of Edinburgh. [NAS]

BEAUQUEINE, ESTINETTE, married Stephen Plant a Frenchman, in Edinburgh on 15 July 1677. [MRE]

BEAUSOLEYLL, JAMES, only son of the late Mathias Beausoleyll a burgess and guilds-brother, was admitted as a burgess and guilds-brother of Edinburgh on 1 June 1625. [EBR]

BEAUZAVILLE, JOHN BAPTISTE, minister of the French congregation in Edinburgh 1746, whose testament was confirmed on 16 May 1771 with the Commissariat of Edinburgh. [NAS][PHS.XLII.xiv]

BECILLY, JAMES, married Mary Knight, in Liberton on 19 August 1791. [MRL]

BEDFORD, JACOB, a cabinetmaker was admitted as a burgess of the Canongate on 27 September 1677. [CBR]

BEGINOT, CHRISTIAN, married Daniel McRaill, in Edinburgh on 20 October 1700. [MRE]

BELFAM, MARGARET, wife of Nicolas Hood a painter, was buried in Greyfriars, Edinburgh, on 18 March 1695. [Greyfriars Burial Register]

BELLANGE, ADRIAN HENRY, a printer in North Kirk parish, married Mary, daughter of James Young a weaver in Lasswade, in Edinburgh on 16 June 1720. [MRE]

BELSONER, ROBERT, married Jean Dick, in Canongate on 16 June 1691. [MRC]

BENAZECK, Madame, a French teacher at Madame Le Blanc's Boarding School in Cant's Close, Edinburgh, 1752. [GED.7]

BERENGER, DAVID, married Magdalene de Bouche, widow of David Juilar, in the Canongate on 18 May 1723. [MRC]

BERENGER, ROBERT, servant of Charles Leroy, weaver in Picardy, Edinburgh, around 1745. [ECA.EBR.MB#vi.162.6279]

BERGER, PAUL, a Frenchman, married Eupham Wilson, in Edinburgh on 23 November 1666. [MRE]

BERIN, NICOL, a merchant in Edinburgh, 1620. [RPCS.XII.764]

BERION, ..., a French Protestant galarian, 1717. [NAS.GD135.141.11.1]

BERNARD, GUILLIAM, a merchant, who was admitted as a burgess and guilds-brother of Edinburgh on 4 September 1583 by right of his wife Katherine, daughter of Hew Brown. [EBR]

BERNARD, PETER, an Ensign of Brigadier James Ferguson's Regiment of Foot, whose testament was confirmed on 14 November 1712 with the Commissary of Edinburgh. [NAS]

BERNARDOU, JACQUES, a Frenchman who was licensed as a schoolmaster in Edinburgh, teaching French, dancing, and fencing, on 2 June 1662. [ECA.EBR]

BICHET, HECTOR, in Dryburgh, 1667. [RGS.XI.1035]

BICHET, JOHN, a bonnet-maker, son of John Bichet a bonnet-maker burgess, was admitted as a burgess of the Canongate on 5 August 1647. [CBR]

BIGORT, MARIE, servant to Lady Jean Dunlop Ralston, in Edinburgh, 1694. [EPT]

BINET, JAMES, a native of Poitiou, France, was naturalised in Scotland 1707. [APS.XI.485]

BISCILLAY, CICILL, married Alexander Park a servant, in Edinburgh on 27 June 1718. [MRE]

BISHOP, GABRIEL, from Maeson, Flanders, then in Norwich to come to Scotland, 1601. [ECA.EBR.MB#vii.209/7550]

BISHOP, JAMES, meil-maker in Cannonmills, husband of Agnes Masson, 1698. [NAS.RD3.90.168]

BLANC, DOROTHEA, married John Scott a cabinet-maker, in Edinburgh on 24 July 1748. [MRE]

BLANC, JOHN, a merchant in North Parish, married Rebecca, daughter of Alexander Wachope of Stotinecleugh, Oldhamstocks parish, in Edinburgh on 14 July 1721. [MRE]

BLANC, LOUIS, a merchant who was admitted as a burgess and guilds-brother of Edinburgh on 16 June 1725. [EBR]

BLAND, HUMPHREY, Lieutenant General, late Governor and Constable of Edinburgh Castle, whose testament was confirmed on 29 September 1763 with the Commissary of Edinburgh. [NAS]

BLAND, JOHN, a Lieutenant of Colonel Richard Cunningham's Regiment of Scots Dragoons in 1695. [DAL.IV.61]

BLANZAY, FRANCIS, a Frenchman, servant to the Duke of Lauderdale, who was admitted as a burgess and guildsbrother of Edinburgh on 7 January 1674. [EBR]

BOBAT, JAMES, a hatmaker, who was admitted as a burgess of Edinburgh on 28 August 1678 by right of his wife Margaret, daughter of Gavin Hamilton a pewterer burgess. [EBR]

BOCHARD, FRANCOIS, a silk weaver, nephew of Nicolas D'Assauville, with his wife Jeanne Masse, and children, from Picardy but resident in Nicolas Street, Spittlefields, London, from there by ship to Sunderland then to Edinburgh in 1730, settled in Candlemaker Row, he introduced the manufacture of cambric to Edinburgh in 1730, returned to London and joined the congregation of Threadneedle Street Church in 1736, his wife died soon after and he remarried, Francois died in 1749. [PHS.XXVII.100/105]

BOCHARD, JOHN, from Picardy to London, then by sea to Sunderland, and overland to Edinburgh, died in January 1730. [PHS.XXVII.101]

BODELIE, JOHN, a hat maker, was admitted as a burgess of the Canongate on 9 February 1655. [CBR]

BODIL, J., drum-major of the 1st Battalion of the Royal Regiment of Foot in 1705. [DAL.V.34]

BOG, JOHN, an archer of the Scots Guards of France during the 1560s. [NAS.NRAS.0.143]

BONENFANT, THEODORE, servant to Hugh, Earl of Loudoun, was admitted as a burgess of Edinburgh on 29 June 1726. [EBR]

BONIGENT, FRANCIS, a stamper burgess, married Janet Acheson, daughter of late William Acheson in Edinburgh, in the Canongate on 1 January 1705. [MRC]

BONNAR, WILLIAM, ensign of Colonel George MacCartney's Regiment of Foot 29 January 1704. [DAL.V.224]

BORELL, JOHAN DE MAUREGNAULT, secretary of Campvere, was admitted as a burgess and guilds-brother of Edinburgh on 4 January 1749. [EBR]

BORIE, FRANCIS, Gentleman of HM Lifeguards, was naturalised in Scotland, 1707. [APS.XI.485]

BOSANQUET, JACOB, a merchant in Hamburg, was admitted as a burgess and guilds-brother of Edinburgh on 19 September 1744. [EBR]

BOSSUGNE, or **BOSSOGUE, JEREMIAH,** was commissioned Adjutant of Major General Maitland's Regiment on 25 August 1702, [DAL.V.222]; and was naturalised in Scotland in 1707. [APS.XI.484]

BOUCHARD, WILLIAM, a gardener, was admitted as a burgess and guilds-brother of Edinburgh on 2 September 1726. [EBR]

BOUISSE, JOHN, Professor of Rhetoric at the University of Caen, was admitted as a burgess of St Andrews in September 1768. [StABR]

BOULER, ..., soldier of Captain St Pierre's troop in Dumfries 1689. [RPCS.XIV.681]

BOULLAY, PETER, was commissioned surgeon of the First Battalion of the Royal Regiment of Foot on 10 November 1688, and was present at the battle of Blenheim in 1705; surgeon of the Second Battalion of the Royal Regiment of Foot in 1709. [DAL.V.34/51/323]

BOURCHIER, WILLIAM, a feuar in Abbeyhill, was admitted as a burgess and guilds-brother of Edinburgh on 26 April 1727. [EBR]

BOYD, JEANNE ELISABETH, daughter of John Boyd, a Scottish merchant in Bordeaux, and his wife Jane, married the Huguenot soldier Jacob de Pechels from Mountaubon, around 1690s. [PHS.XXVII.694]

BRETIER, JEAN, born 1764, from Normandy, formerly resident in Jersey, a student of physic in Edinburgh in 1795. [ECA.Aliens Register]

BRIOT, NICOLAS, to be brought, with servants, to Scotland, 20 February 1632. [RGS.VIII.1929]

BRISCATT, THOMAS, a tailor, husband of ... Paterson, was admitted as a burgess and freeman of Glasgow on 29 October 1594. [GBR]

BRISCOE, ABRAHAM, a hat-maker in Hamilton, was admitted as a burgess and guilds-brother of Glasgow on 9 February 1715. [GBR]

BROCHART, FRANCIS, a weaver of Cambric from Picardy, France, was admitted as a burgess and guilds-brother of Edinburgh on 5 August 1730. [EBR]

BROCKENOGHE, PETER, a waulker and scourer of cloth in Edinburgh, 1601. [ECA.EBR.MB#vii.209/7553]

BRUCE, JAMES, Lieutenant of Major General Maitland's Regiment, and his sons Peter and Frederick, were naturalised in Scotland in 1707. [APS.XI.484]

BRUMMIAD, ..., a French Protestant minister in Edinburgh before June 1717. [ECA.EBR.44.101]

BRUNO, JOHN, in Avignon, brother of James Brun in Edinburgh, 1607. [NAS.RH15.29.64]

BRUSSAT, ANTHONY, a surgeon who was admitted as a freeman of Edinburgh on 4 September 1549. [EBR]

BRUSSAT, ANTHONY, a burgess of Edinburgh, 1643. [NAS.RS.Edinburgh.31/465]

BRUSSET, THOMAS, in Bristo, Edinburgh, 1666. [RGS.XI.898/1022]

BUCCELLIS, CLAUDE, a French music teacher in Edinburgh 1627. [ECA.EBR.26.1.1627]

BUCHAT, JOHN, in Scryne, Panbride, Angus, 16 February 1622. [RGS.VIII.280]

BUKENOGO, PETER, a litster, married Katherine Steilp, in Edinburgh on 6 February 1605. [MRE]

BURBAUX, THOMAS, a sailor or coxswain aboard the Unicorn, whose testament was confirmed on 10 October 1707 with the Commissary of Edinburgh. [NAS]

BURGOUN, JAMES, a hat-maker, who was admitted as a burgess on 22 September 1619 as husband of Christian, daughter of William Tait a merchant burgess. [EBR]

BURJAUD, JOHN, Captain of Colonel Grant's Regiment, was naturalised in Scotland in 1707. [APS.XI.484]

BURNETT, GEORGE, born at Epinay in Champagne, son of George Burnett from Aberdeen, a Huguenot denisized in England and commissioned as a Captain in 1699. [PHS.XXVII.695]

BUSIGA, JEREMIAH, Adjutant of the Earl of Leven's Regiment of Foot in 1693. [DAL.III.334]

BUTHELL, DAVID, servant to James Airth, NP, a witness in Balcaskie, Fife, on 15 September 1632. [RGS.VIII.2140]

BYSCHOP, GABRIEL, a clothworker from Flanders via Norwich who settled in Scotland during 1601. [ECA.EBR; 28.8.1601]

CABANE, ETIENNE, member of the French church in Edinburgh 1713. [ECA.EBR.17.4.1713]

CABELIAU, ZACHARIAS, Major of Colonel Sir William Douglas's Regiment, 1698. [NAS.RD3.89.477]

CADOUR, ANTONY, was commissioned as a Captain of Lord Lorne's Regiment of Foot on 10 July 1697. [DAL.IV.187]

CADOUR, JOHN, was commissioned Captain of Major General Maitland's Regiment on 25 August 1702, [DAL.V.222]; and was naturalised in Scotland in 1707. [APS.XI.484]

CAGNEOLIE, MARGARET, wife of Sir John Scott of Newburgh, 1642. [NAS.RS.Edinburgh.30/167]

CALLIART, DANIEL, a native of Rouen, was admitted as a burgess and guilds-brother of Edinburgh on 22 June 1687. [EBR]

CAMMERT, JOHN, late master of the Royal Academy of Edinburgh, whose testament was confirmed on 12 September 1781 with the Commissary of Edinburgh. [NAS]

CAMPAGNE, DANIEL, sometime Ensign, then Lieutenant of Portmore's Regiment, whose testament was confirmed on 17 June 1724 with the Commissary of Edinburgh. [NAS]

CARBONIER, NICHOLAS, an embroiderer, was admitted as a burgess of Edinburgh on 5 February 1566. [EBR]

CARINE, FRANCIS, born in Doli, France, a valet in Edinburgh Castle, 1794. [ECA.Aliens Register]

CARLIER, JOHN, married Bethia Gibson in Canongate on 11 December 1742, and were parents of Magdalene baptised in St Cuthbert's, Edinburgh, on 13 September 1744. [MRC][BRStC]

CARLIER, JOHN, married Elizabeth Gardener in St Cuthbert's, Edinburgh, on 7 December 1781. [MRStC]

CARLIER, MARY ANN, or MARION, married William Anderson in St Cuthbert's, Edinburgh, on 25 June 1751. [MRStC]

CARLIER, THOMAS, a weaver, with Marion Proy his wife, and their children Francis an 18 year old weaver, John a 10 year old learner weaver, Marion aged 4, and Thomas aged 2, from Picardy via Tournai and Rotterdam bound for Leith, arrived there on 10 October 1729, settled in Candlemaker Row, Edinburgh; was admitted as a burgess and guilds-brother of Edinburgh on 5 August 1730. [EBR][PHS.XXVII.101]

CARLIER, WILLIAM, married Christian Bremner in Edinburgh on 9 April 1806, and were parents of Janet baptised in South Leith on 27 February 1807, David baptised on 20 May 1812, and Richard baptised on 23 April 1814,both in Canongate. [MRE][BRSL][BRC]

CARPENTER, ALEXANDER, was admitted as a burgess and guilds-brother of Edinburgh on 27 November 1556. [EBR]

CARPENTER, Lieutenant WILLIAM, was admitted as a burgess and guilds-brother of Edinburgh on 12 December 1655. [EBR]

CARROULT, or CARRAW, PETER, was commissioned as a Lieutenant of the Earl of Leven's Regiment of Foot on 29 August 1689. He was killed at the storming of Terra Nova, Namur, on 20 August 1695. [DAL.III.85/86]

CARTERET, Captain PHILIP, commander of H.M.S. Harwich, was admitted as a burgess and guilds-brother of Edinburgh on 16 May 1744. [EBR]

CAURAT, PETER, a card-maker in Edinburgh, 1601.
[EBR.MB#vii.209/7555]

CAUVIN, LOUIS, a teacher of French and a heritor in the barony
of Restalrig, 1771, 1775. [NAS.RS27.195.220; 217.265];
1773, [NAS.CS27.8215]; a teacher of French in Edinburgh,
whose testament was confirmed on 4 December 1778 with the
Commissariat of Edinburgh. [NAS]

CAVALIER, ABRAHAM, a surgeon who was admitted as a
burgess of Edinburgh on 30 August 1641. [EBR]

CAVALIER, Captain JAMES, a Lieutenant of the Royal Scots
Dragoons in 1694, [DAL.III.357]; a Lieutenant of HM Troop
of Horse Grenadiers, was naturalised in Scotland in 1707.
[APS.XI.484]

CAVALRIE, ANTHONY, a Frenchman, married Jean Kennedy, in
Edinburgh on 22 January 1667. [MRE]

CAVE, JOSEPH, engraver to the Mint, was admitted as a burgess
and guilds-brother of Edinburgh, by right of his wife Mary,
daughter of Sir Robert Cheislie late Lord Provost of
Edinburgh, on 16 December 1713; whose testament was
confirmed on 16 July 1756 with the Commissary of
Edinburgh. [EBR][NAS]

CAVERT, JOHN, trooper of Colonel Anthony Heyford's Dragoons
in Dumfries, 1689. [RPCS.XIV.680]

CAWPAITH, BLANCHE, married George Thomson, in the
Canongate on 5 July 1608. [CMR]

CAZETTES, ALEXANDER, a Lieutenant of Sir William
Douglas's Regiment of Foot in 1696. [DAL.IV.157]

CHALLENGART, MARGARET, married Hew Kerr, in
Canongate on 9 October 1671. [MRC]

CHAMBEAUX, ADAM, member of the French church in
Edinburgh 1713. [ECA.EBR.17.4.1713]

CHAMBERLAIN, PETER, was admitted as a burgess and guilds-brother of Edinburgh on 14 July 1693. [EBR]

CHAMBERLAIN, PETER, Captain of the <u>Advice</u>, was admitted as a burgess and guilds-brother of Edinburgh on 19 March 1708. [EBR]

CHAMBERLANE, JOSEPH, servant to Lord Ballantyne, was admitted as a burgess and guilds-brother of Edinburgh on 2 February 1670, [EBR]; and his wife Marie Halyburton, were the parents of Joseph who was baptised in Canongate on 7 March 1669. [BRC]

CHAMBON, GASPERT, married Margaret Inglis, in Edinburgh on 23 September 1681. [MRE]

CHAMEAU, FRANCIS, husband of Susanna Pillet, parents of Elizabeth who was baptised in Edinburgh on 15 July 1688. [BRE]

CHAMPAGNE, ..., was commissioned as an Ensign of the Earl of Leven's Regiment of Foot on 29 August 1689. [DAL.III.85]

CHAMPE, JOHN, and his wife Christian Murray, were parents of John who was baptised in South Leith on 25 July 1661. [BRSL]

CHAMPION, JOHN, in Edinburgh, married Agnes or Elizabeth Tock, in Edinburgh on 27 February 1673. [MRE]; parents of Helen baptised 1 February 1674 in Canongate, and John baptised in Edinburgh 19 December 1675. [BRC][BRE]

CHAMPION, JOHN, son in law to the late Isaac Falcon, felt maker, was admitted as a burgess of the Canongate on 5 September 1704, [CBR]; member of the French church in Edinburgh 1713. [ECA.EBR.17.4.1713]

CHAMPION RICHARD, and his wife Elizabeth, were parents of Anna who was baptised in South Leith on 22 May 1660. [BRSL]

CHAMPION DE CRESPIGNY, Captain THOMAS, parish of St James, Westminster, whose testament was confirmed on 10 January 1716 with the Commissary of Edinburgh. [NAS]

CHAMPLAY, WILLIAM, in Jedburgh, 1620. [RPCS.XII.352]

CHANCELLOUR, ALEXANDER, son to the late Robert Chancellour of Seilhill, was apprenticed to James Brown a merchant in Edinburgh on 21 July 1675. [ERA]; a merchant in Edinburgh by 1694. [EPT]

CHANCELLOUR, BARBARA, married Andrew Hamilton, in Canongate on 6 September 1610. [CMR]

CHANCELLOUR, GAVIN, son to the late John Chancellour of Sheilhill, was apprenticed to Simeon Simpson a cordiner in Edinburgh on 22 July 1629. [ERA]

CHANCELLOUR, HELEN, married David Murray a slater, in Edinburgh on 12 November 1712. [MRE]

CHANCELLOUR, HELEN, married James Somervell a wigmaker, in Edinburgh on 7 September 1710. [MRE]

CHANCELLOUR, JOHN, son to the late Robert Chancellour of Sheilhill, was apprenticed to William Chancellour a merchant in Edinburgh on 4 January 1665. [ERA]

CHANCELLOUR, ROBERT, brother of James Chancellour of Shielhill, was apprenticed to James Borthwick a surgeon in Edinburgh on 21 May 1673. [ERA]

CHANCELLOUR, SARAH, married Alexander Hunter, in Edinburgh on 21 September 1721. [MRE]

CHANCELLOUR, WILLIAM, married Janet Stevenson, in Canongate on 27 January 1606. [CMR]

CHANCELLOUR, WILLIAM, late servant to John Chancellour a merchant burgess, was apprenticed to John Carmichael a barber and periwig-maker in Edinburgh on 22 June 1698. [ERA]

CHANELAY, SAMUEL, was admitted as a burgess of the Canongate on 1 May 1673. [CBR]

CHANTENEY, ANTONY, and his wife Mary Reid, were parents of Elizabeth baptised on 6 May 1794, Jean baptised 8 October 1795, and Mary Antoinette baptised 14 December 1796, all in Edinburgh. [BRE]

CHANTRIE, EDWARD, and his wife Euphan Berrie, were parents of Edward who was baptised in Musselburgh on 16 September 1771. [BRM]

CHARANTON, PETER, Captain of Peacock's Regiment, 1714. [NAS.RD3.141.25]

CHARLES, GEORGE, a butcher in Musselburgh, was admitted as a burgess of Edinburgh on 18 July 1753. [EBR]

CHARLES, LEONARD, a pasment worker, married Catherine d'Plancas, in Edinburgh on 26 December 1622. [MRE]

CHARLES, MARY, married James Rodger, in Edinburgh on 26 July 1687. [MRE]

CHARLET, CHARLES ANTOINE, a cambric weaver of Temple le Guerard, arrived in Edinburgh during November 1733, initially he settled in Picardy Place and later in Gorgie, but in 1737 he moved to London where he joined the Threadneedle Street Church, he died in 1759. [PHS.XXVII.105]

CHARLET, JAMES, a weaver, with his wife Margaret Fleming, the daughter of Anne Dassauville and niece of Nicolas Dassauville, and son James aged 2, from Picardy via Tournai and Rotterdam bound for Leith, arrived there on 10 October 1729, second son George Augustus was born on 11 October 1729, settled in Candlemaker Row, Edinburgh; was admitted as a burgess and guilds-brother of Edinburgh on 5 August 1730. [EBR][PHS.XXVII.100]

CHARLEY, JANET, married Robert Wilson in Cramond on 2 July 1674. [MRCramond]

CHARLEY, LANERT, married Katreine De Plantue, in Edinburgh on 26 December 1622. [MRE]

CHARLOT, ANN, married James Lumsdean, in St Cuthbert's, Edinburgh, on 8 January 1773. [MRSt C]

CHARLOT, ANN, married James Thomson, in North Leith, on 14 January 1820. [MRSL]

CHARLOT, ANN, married John Henderson, in St Cuthbert's, Edinburgh, on 9 September 1799. [MRSt C]

CHARLOT, CHARLES, married Mary Somerville, in St Cuthbert's, Edinburgh, on 27 March 1755. [MRStC]

CHARLOT, Captain DANIEL, was commissioned Brigadier of HM Scots Troop of Life Guards on 25 August 1702, [DAL.V.217]; and was naturalised in Scotland during 1707. [APS.XI.484]

CHARLOT, JAMES, married Marion Pringle, in St Cuthbert's, Edinburgh, on 8 April 1769. [MRStC]

CHARLOT, JAMES, married Mariy Ann O'Neill, in St Cuthbert's, Edinburgh, on 6 October 1795. [MRStC]

CHARONTON, PETER, Ensign of Lord Strathnaver's Regiment, was naturalised in Scotland during 1707. [APS.XI.484]

CHARTERS, ALEXANDER, a merchant in Paris, 1670. [NAS.RD4]

CHARTRIES, FRANCIS, a gentleman, Parliament Close, Edinburgh, 1752. [GED.11]

CHASTANE, HENRY, servant of Sir Alexander Hay, a witness in 1611. [RGS.VIII.1507]

CHATENAY, ANTHONY, a French teacher, who was admitted as a burgess and guilds-brother of Edinburgh by right of his wife Marian, daughter of Alexander Reid a merchant burgess and guilds-brother in May 1797. [EBR]

CHAVIUM, SEGAR, a journeyman jeweller in South West parish, married Margaret, daughter of George Baillie a merchant in Inverness, in Edinburgh on 6 August 1749. [MRE]

CHAZELON, PATRICK or PETER, a furrier and a French Protestant refugee, was admitted as a burgess of Edinburgh on 1 July 1696, with permission to import furs and teach apprentices, [EBR]; a furrier burgess of Edinburgh, married Janet, daughter of the late Patrick Graham a skinner burgess there, in Edinburgh on 11 December 1698. [MRE]; parents of David baptised 2 January 1700, Janet baptised 14 January 1701, Isobel baptised 10 December 1701, and Peter baptised 22 April 1703, all in Edinburgh. [BRE]; a glover, skinner and furrier in Edinburgh, 1714. [NAS.RD3.143.284; RD4.114.353]

CHENABOW, ADAM, an interpreter with the weaver from Picardy settled in Edinburgh circa 1730. [OEC.XXV.7]

CHENTER, HENRY, and his wife Mary White, were parents of Jean baptised in Musselburgh on 27 August 1738. [BRM]

CHESNIE, MARION, married Robert Paterson, in Edinburgh on 9 August 1664. [MRE]

CHESSER, ROBERT, a merchant, was admitted as a burgess of Edinburgh on 14 August 1745. [EBR]

CHESSNY, ANTHONY, a joiner, married Helen Smellie a widow, in Edinburgh on 19 January 1779. [MRE]

CHESSNY, ANTHONY, a gravedigger, married Jean Finlay, in Edinburgh on 4 November 1794. [MRE]

CHEVALIER, JEAN, married Victorie Ursula Joseph Bishops, daughter of Louis Bernard Bishops a farmer in St Homers, France, in Edinburgh on 4 January 1797. [MRE]

CHEVALIER, ..., was commissioned Sub-Lieutenant of the 2nd Scots Troop of Horse Grenadier Guards on 6 March 1708. [DAL.V.207]

CHEVIVIX, SARAH, married Hugh Tuite, in Edinburgh on 8 November 1792. [MRE]

CHINYBOW, JOHN, a wigmaker who was admitted as a burgess of Edinburgh on 9 March 1743. [EBR]; married (1) Sarah, daughter of Walter Cochrane in Aberdeen, in Edinburgh on 21 April 1745, (2) Elizabeth, daughter of Thomas Gordon in Leith, in Edinburgh on 4 November 1750. [MRE]

CHRISTIEN, MARGARET, married James Brodie a peuterer, in Edinburgh on 24 October 1708. [MRE]

CLARIHUE, JOHN, servant to James Steedman a vintner in North Kirk parish, married Janet, daughter of Thomas Gibson a litster in Inverness, in Edinburgh on 1 March 1741. [MRE]

CLASEN, JACOB, a weaver from Maeson, Flanders, then in Norwich bound for Scotland, 1601. [EBR.MB#vii.209/7551]

CLASEN, JAMES, a slater in North East kirk parish, married Isobel, daughter of Alexander Mathison a brewer in North East parish, in Edinburgh on 28 December 1716. [MRE]

CLAUDE, ..., ..., a French Protestant in Utrecht, 1716. [NAS.GD135.141.7.7]

CLENTYN, HENRY, Duc d'Oysell, was admitted as a burgess and guilds-brother of Edinburgh on 10 January 1558. [EBR]

CLERIHUE, JOHN, a vintner, was admitted as a burgess and guilds-brother of Edinburgh on 24 January 1759. [EBR]

CLINQUAN, SEBASTIEN, a Walloon from Tournai alias Doornik, proposed to the Town Council of Edinburgh that he would settle there and manufacture damask napery, woollen damask, tapestry, figured velvets, braids and other material, 1601. [EBR.MB.vii.209/7554]

COBZIER, PETER, an Exciseman, in Cowgate Head South, Edinburgh, 1752. [GED.12]

COINDEL, JEAN FRANCOIS, a medical student, married Catherine, daughter of Charles Walker a vintner, in Edinburgh on 24 October 1796. [MRE]

COMBETES, ..., a French Protestant galarian, 1717. [NAS.GD135.141.11.1]

COMPANION, ELIZABETH, married George Tarbert, in Canongate on 11 November 1659. [MRC]

COMPANION, MARGARET, married James Wilson, in Edinburgh on 5 March 1607. [MRE]

CONDOMIE, ELIZABETH, married Lawrence Graham, both of West Kirk if Edinburgh parish, in Canongate on 8 December 1646. []

CONSIGNE, JAMES, a cordiner burgess and freeman of the Canongate, contracted to marry Margaret Johnston, servant to John Hamilton their Majesty's baillie in the Abbey of Holyroodhouse, on 13 May 1693, but the marriage did not occur. []

CONTENOT, JOHN, journeyman goldsmith, resident with James Penman a goldsmith in Edinburgh, 1694. [EPT]

CORSANDER, JOHN, late servant to William Chrystie a stabler, married Janet Sinclair widow of William Park a horse hirer, in Canongate on 14 July 1698. []

COSSAERT, DAVID, a merchant in Bordeaux, 1674-1690. [NAS.RH15.59.6]

COSSARD, THOMAS, an apprentice to Patrick Anderson a wright in Edinburgh, 1694. [EPT]

COSSART, ABRAHAM, in Rouen, 1684. [NAS.GD277, Box 11, bundle 6]

COSSART, ISAAC, in Edinburgh, 1691. [RPCS.XVI.614]

COSSENOT, Mrs, Trunk Close, Edinburgh, 1752. [GED.13]

COSSIER, SIMON, a painter, married Christian Esplin, in Edinburgh on 13 September 1787. [MRE]

COUDET, THOMAS, son of the late George Coudet a burgess of Musselburgh, was apprenticed to James Wright a wright in Edinburgh on 8 December 1658. [ERA]

COULLEY, JOHN, an Ensign of Morrison's Regiment of Foot was admitted as a burgess and guilds-brother of Glasgow on 9 March 1716. [GBR]

COURTEOUS, RICHARD, a smith in South Kirk parish, married Isobel, daughter of William Darline, in North East parish, in Edinburgh on 26 November 1702. [MRE]

COURTRIE, ALEXANDER, son of the late Patrick Courtrie in Lasswade, was apprenticed to Thomas Girdwood a tailor in Edinburgh on 23 September 1668. [ERA]

COURTRIE, JEAN, married Stephen Forrester a basketmaker, in Edinburgh on 5 November 1732. [MRE]

COUSINAN, ELIZABETH, married Alexander Cameron a writer in Edinburgh, in Canongate on 11 March 1735. []

COUSINAN, JOHN, secretary to the Salt Office in Edinburgh, whose testament was confirmed on 29 July 1726 with the Commissary of Edinburgh. [NAS]

COUSTEIL, WILLIAM, a merchant and a vintner in Edinburgh, whose testament was confirmed on 21 December 1744, and 25 January 1751, with the Commissary of Edinburgh. [NAS]

COUSTEILL, ALEXANDER, a wigmaker was admitted as a burgess and guilds-brother by right of his father Peter Cousteill a tailor burgess and guilds-brother on 31 May 1728. [EBR]; married Margaret, daughter of John Douglas a tailor burgess in Fisher-row, in Edinburgh on 1 June 1729. [MRE]

COUSTEILL, JOHN, son of Peter Cousteill a tailor in the Canongate, was apprenticed to Paul Roumieu a watchmaker in Edinburgh on 29 August 1694. [ERA]; an apprentice resident with Paul Romieu, 1694, [EPT]; a former apprentice of Paul Roumieu junior in Edinburgh; a watchmaker who was admitted as a burgess and guilds-brother of Edinburgh by right of his father Peter Cousteill on 16 February 1715. [EBR]

COUSTEILL, PIERRE alias PETER, married (1) Margaret Peell, parents of Anna baptised 8 June 1690, Daniel baptised 12 August 1691, and William baptised 8 September 1700, all in Canongate, [BRC]; a member of the French church in Edinburgh 1713. [EBR, 17.4.1713]; a tailor in the Canongate who was admitted as a burgess and guilds-brother of Edinburgh, by right of his wife Barbara, daughter of William Douglas a tailor burgess and guilds-brother, on 16 February 1715, [EBR]; alias La Pearle, a tailor burgess of Edinburgh, his relict Barbara Douglas's testament was confirmed on 5 December 1733 with the Commissary of Edinburgh. [NAS]

COWART, PETER, a Flemish card-maker, with five children, in Edinburgh in 1601. [EBR: 3.11.1601]

COWPLANE, KATHERINE, in the Cowgait, married Thomas Robeson in Edinburgh, there in December 1603. []

CRAMDEN, HENRY, a musician, was naturalised in Scotland 1707. [APS.XI.485]

CREGUT, PETER, formerly a Lieutenant of Sir William Douglas's Regiment, was naturalised in Scotland in 1707. [APS.XI.484]

CRESPIGNY, THOMAS, second son of Claude Champion de Crespigny, was commissioned as Cornet of Lord Cardross's Dragoons on 7 August 1689, [DAL.III.36/134]; Lieutenant of Colonel Richard Cunningham's Regiment of Scots Dragoons in 1695, [DAL.IV.61]; Captain Lieutenant of the Marquis of Lothian's Regiment of Dragoons at Jedburgh on 11 September 1703. [DAL.V.207]

CROCQUIER, ..., in Stirling 1687. [see New Mills Cloth Manufactory, 1631-1703, fo.165]

CUSATTER, VIOLET, married William Aitkin a tailor, in Edinburgh on 6 September 1723. [MRE]

DAILIEIR, JAMES, son of Francis Dailieir a merchant, was buried in Greyfriers Burial ground, Edinburgh, on 19 January 1675. [GBR]

DALATTE, WILLIAM, and his wife Helen Murray, were parents of Helen who was baptised in St Cuthbert's, Edinburgh, on 6 December 1799. [BRStC]

DALHOM, PHILIP JACOB SIXT, sometime Captain of Cunningham's Regiment of Foot, then of Buchan's Regiment, whose testament was confirmed on 31 March 1710 with the Commissary of Edinburgh. [NAS]

DALIDEE, MARGARET, married Thomas Inglis, in Canongate on 14 February 1616. []

DALLET, JOHN, from Picardy to London, then by sea to Sunderland, overland to Edinburgh.; a cambric weaver who was admitted as a burgess and guilds-brother of Edinburgh on 5 August 1730, he died between 1750 and 1762. [EBR][PHS.XXVII.101/105]

DAMARRIS, ANNA, married Jacques de Bussynt in Canongate, in the West Kirk of Edinburgh on 30 June 1601. []

DAMMAN, or **DAMOND, SARA,** married Jacques De La Bare, or La Barge, a merchant, in Edinburgh on 4 January 1604. [MRE]; later resident in Leith, her testament was confirmed on 25 March 1623 with the Commissary of Edinburgh. [NAS]

DANAPLANSIRE, THOMAS, a shipwrecked Frenchman in Leith, 1658. [EBR.MB#vii.186/9]

DANGAND, MARIA, daughter of Charles Dangand a glover in London, married Thomas Boswel a servant, in Canongate on 13 February 1798. []

DANGRAN, JOHN, father of Gilbert who was baptised in Canongate on 24 August 1565. [BRC]

DANGUEL, Monsieur, maitre des comptes, was admitted as a burgess and guilds-brother of Edinburgh on 3 October 1752. [EBR]

DARANDA, PAUL, a merchant in London, whose testament was confirmed on 8 June 1733 with the Commissary of Edinburgh. [NAS]

DARQUIER, Captain PETER, husband of Elizabeth Coustille, parents of Barbara, baptised 31 July 1720, Veronica baptised 30 June 1727, Sarah baptised 4 May 1729, Simon baptised 19 October 1730, Jacob baptised 30 November 1731, Moses baptised 27 December 1734, and Lucy baptised 12 January 1738, all in Musselburgh. [BRM]; late cornet of Brigadier Lapell's Regiment of Dragoons, whose testament was confirmed on 25 July 1739 with the Commissary of Edinburgh. [NAS]

DARTINELL, MARTIN, trumpeter of Lieutenant Colonel Langstone's troop in Dumfries, 1689. [RPCS.XIV.703]

DASKELL, ..., trumpeter of Lieutenant Colonel Langstone's troop in Kirkcudbright, 1689. [RPCS.XIV.703]

DASSAUVILLE, ANN, widow of Hubert Fleming, and her children Katherine, Ann and Jacob, all spinners or weavers, from St Quentin, Picardy, via Tournai and Rotterdam bound for Leith, arrived there on 10 October 1729, settled in Candlemaker Row, Edinburgh, a spinning instructor in Paisley, and in Edinburgh from 1739 to 1762. [EBR.MB#vii.248/7672-7688] [PHS.XXVII.101/102]

DASSAUVILLE, DUNCAN, married Katherine, daughter of George Yule a farmer in Dirleton, in Edinburgh on 18 November 1759, [MRE]; a weaver at Picardy, Edinburgh, 16 April 1777. [NAS.RS27.232.203]; a manufacturer in Picardy, and his wife Katherine Yule, whose testament was confirmed on 14 August 1787 with the Commissariat of Edinburgh. [NAS]

DASSAUVILLE, JOHN, weaver, brother of Nicolas Dassauville, and his wife Francoise Carlier, from St Quentin, Picardy via

Tournai (where they married) and Rotterdam bound for Leith, arrived there on 10 October 1729, settled in Candlemaker Row, Little Picardy, Broughton, parish of St Cuthbert's, Edinburgh; admitted as a burgess and guilds-brother of Edinburgh on 5 August 1730, dead by 1736; whose testament was confirmed on 23 February 1738 with the Commissary of Edinburgh. [EBR][PHS.XXVII.105][NAS]

DASSAUVILLE, JOHN, married Claudia Le Roye, in St Cuthbert's, Edinburgh, on 19 April 1737. [MRStC]

DASSAUVILLE, NICOL, a surgeon-dentist, married Mary, daughter of Captain Alston on the Honourable East India Company Service, in Canongate on 12 November 1800, [MRC]; who was admitted as a burgess and guilds-brother of Edinburgh on 29 October 1817. [EBR]; born 1773, died 17 October 1851. [Dean gravestone, Edinburgh]

DASSAUVILLE, NICOLAS, from St Quentin, Picardy, a cambric weaver, was contracted by the Commissioners for Improving, Fisheries and Manufactures in Scotland to recruit families from France who would introduce the manufacture of cambrics, looms and bleaching in 1727; settled at Picardy Place, Edinburgh, admitted as a burgess and guilds-brother of Edinburgh on 5 August 1730, commissioned stamp-master of cambrics 14 August 1730; master of Andrew Kirkcaldy around 1745; his testament was confirmed on 17 September 1760 with the Commissary of Edinburgh. [NAS] [EBR.MB#vi#162.6279; vii.248.7672/7688] [PHS.XXVII.99]

DAUBER, JAMES, from Norwich, was admitted as a burgess and guilds-brother of Edinburgh on 2 May 1759. [EBR]

DAUBER, RICHARD, secretary of the Commissioner of Excise in Scotland, was admitted as a burgess and guilds-brother of Edinburgh on 15 October 1755. [EBR]

D'AUVERGNE, EDWARD, Chaplain of the Scots Foot Guards in 1693. [DAL.III.309]

DAVILLOURIS, SEBASTIAN, burgess of Edinburgh, sometime commissar clerk thereof, whose testament was confirmed on 20 April 1604 with the Commissariat of Edinburgh. [NAS]

DAVILLOUERT, CLAUDE, son of Sebastian Davillouert, secretary to Mary, Queen of Scots, and his wife Janet Adamson, Edinburgh, 1629. [RGS.VIII.1423]

DEARLON, THOMAS, barber to the Duke of Buccleugh, was admitted as a burgess and guilds-brother of Edinburgh on 2 July 1679. [EBR]

DE BARR, WILLIAM, married Margaret Sandilands or Gib, in South Leith on 10 April 1801. [MRSL]

DEBBUNG, Captain Hugh, in H.M. Service, married Janet Seton, in Edinburgh on 27 March 1763. [MRE]

DE BELLOT, ETIENNE, a Lieutenant of Lord Murray's Regiment of Foot in 1694, died in August 1696. [DAL.III.386]

DE BERRY, PIERRE, a young man from Dieppe in Edinburgh by 1590. [EBR:29.7.1590]

DE BOIS, DESLIS, in Rochelle, was serviced as heir to his uncle Peter Petite a sailmaker in Leith on 27 August 1713. [NAS.S/H]

DE BOIS, JOHN, son of Bartholemew De Bois and his wife Ann Aükier, was baptised in Edinburgh on 26 February 1634. [BRE]

DE BOUCHIE, MAGDALENE, widow of David Juilar, married David Berenger, in Canongate, Edinburgh, on 18 May 1723. [MRC]

DE BOULT, JOHN, and his wife Jean, were parents of Cirsten who was baptised in North Leith on 24 July 1683. [BRNL]

DE BOWSIE, ELIZABETH, wife of James Maxwell of Innerwick, 1642. [NAS.RS.Haddington. 30/149]

DE BUCY. PETER, a French refugee in Edinburgh, around 1694. [ECA.SL1/1/35.57]

DE BURGIE, Colonel, was admitted as a burgess and guilds-brother of Edinburgh on 24 February 1716. [EBR]

DE BUSIER, JACQUES, was the father of Joanna, who was baptised on 10 October 1596, and of William, who was baptised on 22 April 1599, both in Edinburgh. [BRE]

DE BUSSO, Sir FRANCIS, 1647. [NAS.RS.Edinburgh.34/370]

DE BUSSYNT or BUSKINE, JACQUES, married Anna Dammaris or Dammause, both resident in the Canongate, were married at the West Kirk of Edinburgh on 30 June 1601. [MRE]

DE BUTTELLIS, CLAUDE, a French music teacher in Edinburgh, around 1626. [ECA.SL1/1/14/37]

DE CAIRLL, CHRISTIAN, was the parent of James baptised in Edinburgh on 23 July 1595, and of David and William both baptised in Canongate on 4 September 1601. [BRE/BRC]

DE CANTON, JAMES, French master, in Edinburgh, 1680s. [NAS.RD4.81.140]

DE CARPENTIER, Sir JAMES, son of Sir Peter de Carpentier, chief governor of the Dutch East Indies, was admitted as a burgess and guilds-brother of Edinburgh on 31 May 1661. [EBR]

DECHAMP, ..., founder of a papermill at Cathcart and at Upper Spylaw near Colinton, Edinburgh, around 1681. [OEC.XXV.70]

DE CLEVE, JEAN, 1697. [NAS.RD4.81.556]

DE CLEVE, Madame MACHTELSIE, a widow, 1697. [NAS.RD4.81.556]

DE COLLIGNE, HENRIETTA, daughter of Gaspard de Colligne, Marshal of Chatillon, France, and wife of Thomas Hope, Earl of Haddington, 1643. [NAS.RS.Haddington.31/198-200]

DE CORNAT, JOHN, a broker in Bordeaux, was admitted as a burgess of Glasgow on 26 July 1630. [GBR]

DE CORONET, JAMES, from Bordeaux, was admitted as a burgess and guilds-brother of Edinburgh on 30 May 1649. [EBR]

DE CORTE, PAUL, a Flemish dyer arrived in Edinburgh via Norwich in 1601. [ECA.EBR.MB#vii.209/7542]

DECRO, WILLIAM, and his wife Susannah Plant, were the parents of William who was baptised in Edinburgh on 9 April 1718. [BRE]

DEEPIE, ALEXANDER, and his wife Isobel Wilson, were the parents of Isobel baptised 9 December 1694, and John baptised 18 September 1698, both in Carrington. [BRCa]

DEEPIE, DOROTHY, married William Clerk, in South Leith on 7 April 1732. [MRSL]

DEEPIE, ELIZABETH, married David Lindsay, in St Cuthbert's, Edinburgh, on 11 December 1726. [MRStC]

DEEPIE, JANET, married Robert Montgomerie a writer, in Edinburgh on 1 July 1652. [MRE]

DEEPIE, JOHN, and his wife ... Wishart, were parents of a son who was baptised in Carrrington on 11 July 1669. [BRCa]

DEEPIE, ROBERT, and his wife Elizabeth Sergeant, were parents of William who was baptised in Edinburgh on 14 October 1664. [BRE]

DEEPIE, WILLIAM, and his wife Agnes Walker, were the parents of James baptised 2 January 1687, Elizabeth baptised 6 January 1695, Adolphus baptised 29 May 1698, Elizabeth baptised 31 October 1700, Marion baptised 13 June 1704, Margaret baptised 21 February 1706, and Dorothea baptised 8 May 1709, all in South Leith. [BRSL]

DEEPIE, WILLIAM, married Margaret Clephan, in South Leith on 5 July 1720. [MRSL]

D'EFFRENE, Mlle., a dancing mistress, Carruber's Close, Edinburgh, 1752. [GED.15]

DE FIDEL, MICHEL, "left France on account of the troubles" in Edinburgh around 1794 but bound for Philadelphia to see his parents. [ECA.Aliens Register]

DE FOE, DANIEL, a merchant in London, was admitted as a burgess of Glasgow on 12 May 1707. [GBR]

DE FOUR, DOMINICK, a servant of the Duke of Hamilton, was admitted as a burgess and guilds-brother of Glasgow on 15 September 1721. [GBR]

DE FOUR, JOHN, Captain of the Earl of Dunbarton's Regiment, was admitted as a burgess and guilds-brother of Edinburgh on 4 June 1685. [EBR]

DE FRANCE, LOUIS, a music schoolmaster in Edinburgh, 1675. [EBR: 26.3.1675]

DEFRESNE, Mrs M. C. L., wife of William Russell an advocate, died 5 November 1831, buried in St Cuthbert's churchyard, Edinburgh. [St Cuthbert's g/s]

DEGAR, SARA, poor, was buried in Greyfriars burial ground Edinburgh, on 4 May 1695. [GBR]

DE GRAHAVE, ISAAC, was commissioned as surgeon of the Scots Troop of Life Guards on 24 December 1689. [DAL.III.21]

DE GRAVE, DANIEL, surgeon of the Scots Troop of Life Guards, 1694. [DAL.III.350]

DE GRAVE, JACK, servant to Lord Drumlanrig, was admitted as a burgess and guilds-brother of Edinburgh on 2 January 1684. [EBR]

DE HATENVILLE, ..., a child of James Dehatenville a turner, was buried in Greyfriars burial ground, Edinburgh, on 26 June 1694. [GBR]

D'HEARCOURT, LOUIS CLAUDE D'ACHANY, a merchant in St Quintin, bailliage of Vermandois, France, whose testament was confirmed on 12 February 1755 with the Commissariat of Edinburgh. [NAS]

DEHEONER, JANET, a servant of Katherine Inglis the widow of George Cheine late town clerk of Leith, in Edinburgh, 1694. [EPT]

DE HESUE, LAWRENCE, was the father of Gassiott who was baptised in the Canongate on 13 November 1601. [BRC]

DEHEW, JOHN, a carpenter who established a glass-works in Leith by 1689. [RPCS.XIV.382]

DE HINGER, PETER, a cutler in Canongate, husband of Jasmine Buttferance, 1631. [NAS.RS.Edinburgh.18/139-140]

DE HUNGER, CHRISTIAN, daughter of Peter De Hunger, was baptised in Edinburgh on 18 June 1598. [BRE]

DE HUNGER, SARA, daughter of Peter De Hunger, was baptised in Edinburgh on 23 May 1596. [BRE]

DEIPIE, JAMES, son of William Deipie a wright in South Leith, was apprenticed to John Denholm a wright in Edinburgh, on 1 December 1703. [ERA]

DEIPOE, JOHN, an overseer at Edinburgh Castle, 1639 to 1640. [AMW#400-430]

DEIPPA, JOHN, married Isobel Walker, in the Canongate on 24 December 1626, [MRC]; parents of James baptised 31 July 1628, Agnes baptised 9 June 1631, Margaret baptised 31 May 1636, and John baptised 15 December 1639, all in Canongate. [BRC]

DEIPPE, EUPHEMIA, in Edinburgh, married Robert Morison, in the Canongate on 6 April 1647. [MRC]

DE LABADIE, JAMES, page to the Duke of Albany, was\admitted as a burgess and guild-brother of Edinburgh on 10 June 1681. [EBR]

DE LA BARE, FRANCIS, a cooper in London, 1695. [NAS.RD3.LXXXIV.321]

DE LA BARE, JACQUES, a merchant, married Sara Damman, in Edinburgh on 4 January 1604. [MRE]

DE LA BENE, JOHN LOUIS, a Captain of the Earl of Argyll's Regiment of Foot in 1694. [DAL.III.376]

DE LA CLOUSE, ELIZABETH, married John Stirling, in Edinburgh on 15 May 1722. [MRE]

DE LA CLOUSE, ELIZABETH, was serviced as heir to her brother John, son of John De La Clouse a merchant in Forfar, on 10 April 1722. [NAS.S/H]

DE LA FONT, JOHN ABEL, married Katherine Bull, in St Cuthbert's, Edinburgh, on 7 December 1768. [MRStC]

DE LA FONTAINE, JACOB, 1697. [NAS.RD4.81.828]

DE LA FRIZIES, PATRICK, 1714. [NAS.RD2.103.2.3214]

DE LALO, SAMPSON, was commissioned as Captain in Colonel Balcastel's Regiment of French Foot on 2 December 1691, then a Captain Lieutenant in the Scots Guards from 1 July 1697, on 1 May 1702 he was appointed Lieutenant Colonel of Colonel John Gibson's Regiment of Foot, and on 5 February 1704 he became Colonel, in June 1706 he transferred to the Scots Fusiliers, served under Marlborough, became Brigadier General on 1 January 1709, killed at Malplaquet; whose testament was confirmed on 23 June 1715 with the Commissary of Edinburgh. [DAL.IV.171][NAS]

DE LA MERE, MARTIN, of Captain Mordaunt's Company, in Ayr, 1689. [RPCS.XIV.674]

DE LA MOTTE, CHARLES, a merchant from Hull, was admitted as a burgess and guilds-brother of Edinburgh on 14 February 1750. [EBR]

DE LA MOTTE, PIERRE, a dancing master who was admitted as a burgess of Edinburgh on 3 December 1735. [EBR]; a dancing master, Baxter's Close, Edinburgh, 1752. [GED.29]

DE LA MOTTE, WINIFRED, a widow in the parish of St George, Middlesex, 1772. [NAS.RS.Berwick.16/184]

DE LANGE, DAVID, a waulker and scourer of cloth, in Edinburgh, 1601. [ECA.EBR.MB#vii.209.7553]

DE LANGE, PHILIP, a shipmaster, 1705. [NAS.RD3.106.484]

DE LA PORTE, FRANCIS, was admitted as a burgess and guilds-brother of Edinburgh on 26 August 1747. [EBR]

DE LA ROUSE, PETER, a printer, married Marion Fairholm, in Edinburgh on 21 July 1633. [MRE]

DE LARRY, HARRY, Captain of the Prince Royal Regiment of Prussia, was admitted as a burgess and guilds-brother of Glasgow on 29 July 1719. [GBR]

DE LAT, JOHN, a weaver in Picardy Place, Edinburgh, around 1733; whose testament was confirmed on 4 March 1762 with the Commissary of Edinburgh. [PHS.XXVII.102][NAS]

DE LA TOUCAYE, ..., a refugee from France who was in Scotland during the 1790s. [ECA. Aliens Register]

DELATT, WILLIAM, a weaver, married Helen, daughter of Andrew Murray a labourer in Edinburgh, in Canongate on 27 November 1798. [MRC]

DE LATTER, JOHN, a caroline weaver in Picardy, testament confirmed on 4 March 1762 with the Commissariat of Edinburgh. [NAS]

DE LAUNE, Colonel HENRY, in Dublin, whose testament was confirmed on 10 December 1748 with the Commissariat of Edinburgh. [NAS]

DE LAUTER, JOHN, barber to the Duke of Albany and York, was admitted as a burgess and guilds-brother of Edinburgh on 26 December 1679. [EBR]

DE LA VALLE, Captain WILLIAM, and his wife Mary de Gelder, were parents of Joseph who was baptised in Edinburgh on 1 March 1715. [BRE]

DE LAWELL, RODOLPH, a sailor in Leith, husband of Barbara Logan, 1637. [NAS.RS.Edinburgh.26/166]

DE LAWN, BENJAMIN, servant to Lord Brogill, was admitted as a burgess and guilds-brother of Edinburgh on 20 September 1656. [EBR]

DE LENCY, JOHN, and his wife Anne Mackenzie, were parents of John who was baptised in Edinburgh on 24 November 1790. [BRE]

DE LISLE, MARY, married Captain John Ramsay, in Edinburgh on 10 April 1800. [MRE]

DE LISLE, PHILIP, of Calcutta, Bengal, whose testament was confirmed on 4 July 1789 with the Commissary of Edinburgh. [NAS]

DELLAND, Lieutenant, a prisoner in Canongate Tolbooth, 1690. [RPCS.XV.517]

DE LOAN, HENRY, and his wife Louisa Barber, were parents of William who was baptised in Canongate on 19 January 1733. [BRC]

DELUES, Captain ROGER, married Elizabeth Heartlay, in Edinburgh on 22 October 1661. [MRE]

DELUZE, JAMES, Captain of Dragoons, was admitted as a burgess and guilds-brother of Glasgow on 9 January 1716. [GBR]

DE MALIVERNE, ANNA, wife of Dr George Sibbald. 1632, 1634. [NAS.RS.Edinburgh.19/122; 22/284]

DE MALIVERNE, ANNA, widow of Robert Boyd of Trochrig, 1646. [NAS.RS1 {Ayr}.555.452]; whose testament was confirmed on 14 December 1654 with the Commissariat of Edinburgh. [NAS]

DE MANSELL, CHARLES, servant of Lord Robert Burley, and husband of Margaret Melvill, 1623. [NAS.RS1[Fife].13.358]

DE MANSELL, CHARLES, was granted lands in Perthshire and in Clackmannanshire on 24 March 1664. [RGS.XI.580]

DE MARSILLERS, PIERRE, a Huguenot pastor who taught Greek in Montrose, Angus, during the early 1600s. [PHS.XXVII.699]

DE MAUSS, CHARLES, servant to Robert, Lord Burleigh, husband of Margaret Melville, 1651. [NAS.RS.Fife, #xviii.121]

DE MEE, JOHN, 1697. [NAS.RD4.81.604, 731]

DE METER, ..., was commissioned as an Ensign of the Scots Foot Guards in September 1691. [DAL.III.190]

DE MILLON, JOHN, was commissioned as a Captain Lieutenant of the Earl of Argyll's Regiment of Foot in 1693, later Captain of Colonel Robert Mackay's Regiment of Fusiliers on 1 October 1696. [DAL.III.337;IV.138]

DE MONT, JOHN, a pensioner of the Royal Artillery, married Ann, daughter of David Gellatly a cook, in Canongate on 4 March 1790. [MRC]

DE MONTREILL, JEAN, Senator of Louis XIV of France, was admitted as a burgess of Old Aberdeen on 22 May 1647. [OABR]

DE MONTRESOR, JACQUES GABRIEL, born 1668, son of Jacques de Tresor, was commissioned as Ensign of the Scots Foot Guards on 1 September 1691, Lieutenant in 22 May 1694, Captain of the Royal Scots Fusiliers 25 February 1702, was wounded at Malplaquet, later Major of the Scots Fusiliers and Governor of Fort William, Scotland, died there on 29 January 1724. [DAL.III.192; V.80]

DE MONTY, SAMUEL, surgeon's mate of the Royal Regiment of Foot at the Battle of Blenheim in 1705. [DAL.V.33]

DE MYEARNE, THEODORE, H.M.Physician, was admitted as a burgess and guilds-brother of Edinburgh on 27 June 1617. [EBR]

DENAINE, JANET, wife of James Middleton an armourer, was buried in Greyfriars burial ground, Edinburgh, on 22 September 1684. [GBR]

DENEIN, DAVID, the elder, a saddler in the Canongate, 1691. [NAS.RD2.72.770]

DENEVALL, GEORGE, married Helen Ballentyne, in Musselburgh on 21 September 1711. [MRM]; parents of George baptised 8 May 1715, and Anna baptised 6 October 1717, both in Musselburgh. [BRM]

DENEVALL, ISOBEL, married James Key a servant, in Edinburgh on 16 June 1709. [MRE]

DENEVALL, JANET, married Alexander Letham, in Edinburgh on 11 October 1747. [MRE]

DENEVALL, JOHN, a cabinetmaker, married Anne Black, in Edinburgh on 16 June 1780. [MRE]

DE NICOLAY, ..., 1707. [NAS.RD2.94.489]

DENIS, PIERRE FRANCIS, valet de chamber to General William Cadogan, was admitted as a burgess and guilds-brother of Glasgow on 7 May 1716. [GBR]

DENISE, CLAUDIUS, a merchant in London, 1683, a gentleman in London, 1698, 1702. [NAS.RD4.56.353; RD3.57.246; RD3.57.363; RD3.87.755; RD3.99.1.215]; whose testament was confirmed on 5 February 1706 with the Commissary of Edinburgh. [NAS]

DENISE, STEPHEN, in London, 1698. [NAS.RD2.81.2.407]

DENNEIS, HENRIE, married Janet Grant, in Edinburgh on 19 January 1658. [MRE]

DENNIVALL, WILLIAM, a toolmaker, married Anne Robertson from Dunfermline, in Edinburgh on 23 June 1798. [MRE]

DEN TURK, HENRY, from Maeson, Flanders, then in Norwich to come to Scotland, 1601. [ECA.EBR.MB#vii.209/7551]

DE PLANCAS, CATHERINE, married Charles Leonard a pasment worker, in Edinburgh on 26 December 1622, [MRE]

DE PLANCAS, KATHERINE, married Henrik Stallen, in South Leith on 24 November 1600. [MRSL]

DE PLANCAS, MAGDALENE, married Robert Galbraith in South Leith on 26 November 1692. [MRSL]

DE PLANQUAS, ELIAS, stifing maker in Leith, testament confirmed on 28 May 1621 with the Commissariat of Edinburgh. [NAS]

DE PLANQUAS, ELIAS, in Leith, 1648-1650, [NAS.RS.Edinburgh.35/353; 37/2; 38/37]

DE PLANQUAS, ELIZABETH, daughter of Elias De Planquas, in Leith, widow of Hugh Tod a Writer to the Signet, 1648- 1659. [NAS.RS.Edinburgh.35/353;36/138; 37/2; 38/37; 8/201]

DE PLANTUE, KATREINE, married Lanert Charley, in Edinburgh on 26 December 1622. [MRE]

DE PLEINE, HENRY, and his wife Barbara Smith, were parents of Margaret who was baptised in South Leith on 16 June 1616. [BRDL]

DEPOMER, Mrs, a Frenchwoman, wife of James Depomer, was buried in Greyfriars burial ground, Edinburgh, on 28 October 1689. [GBR]

DEPPO, HENRY, in Langshaw, 1606. [RGS.I7]

DEPPO, JOHN, servant to Euphane Wilson, was admitted as a burgess of the Canongate on 12 June 1628. [CBR]

DEPPO, ROBERT, marriage contract dated October 1663; married Elizabeth Sergeant in South Leith on 24 December 1663, [MRSL]; was admitted as a burgess of the Canongate by right of his wife, the daughter of William Sergeant an upholsterer burgess, 2 February 1671. [CBR]; his testament was confirmed in 1676 with the Commissariat of Edinburgh, [NAS]; he was buried in Greyfriars churchyard in Edinburgh. [Greyfriars g/s]

DEPPO, WILLIAM, son of Robert Deppo a burgess, was admitted as a burgess of the Canongate on 11 August 1694. [CBR]

DE PRADES, TERSON, a French Protestant in Toulouse, applied to settle in Great Britain on 8 April 1716. [NAS.GD135.141.7.47]

DE PYEL, CHRISTIAN, from Maeson, Flanders, then in Norwich to come to Scotland, 1601; petition dated 1614. [ECA.EBR.MB#vii.209/7551, 7651, 7572]

DE RAMSAY, LOUIS, a Huguenot of Scots descent, born at Luman in Orleans, joined the Dutch Army after 1685, commissioned in a Huguenot regiment in England 1689, granted denization in 1688. [PHS.XXVII.695]

DE RIZIE, MATTHEW, Captain of the 6th Regiment, was admitted as a burgess of St Andrews on 2 June 1766. [StABR]

DERTIGUES, PETER, a journeyman goldsmith in Old Kirk parish, Edinburgh, 1694. [EPT]

DESAGUILIERS, Reverend Dr JOHN THEOPHILUS, was admitted as a burgess and guilds-brother of Edinburgh on 18 January 1721. [EBR]

DESBOIERT, DESLIS, a Protestant refugee in Edinburgh, 1697. [NAS.RD4.80.1061]

DESCHAMPES, NICOLAS, a paper-man at Dalray Mills, 1681. [NAS.RD3.54.533]

DES GRANGES, DAVID, born 1611, son of Sampson des Granges and his wife Marie Bouvier, baptised in London as a Huguenot in 1611 or 1613, artist to Charles II in Scotland around 1651, died 1675. [PS#43]

DESHAN, NICHOLAS, was admitted as a burgess of Glasgow on 15 April 1693. [GBR]

DESPEARE, WILLIAM, Captain of Sir William Douglas's Regiment of Foot, was admitted as a burgess and guilds-brother of Glasgow on 5 April 1694. [GBR]

DES ROMANES, JAMES, was commissioned as Lieutenant of Colonel John Gibson's Regiment of Foot on 9 April 1696. [DAL.IV.151]

DESPIERRES, Captain WILLIAM, 1697. [NAS.RD4.81.1371]

DESPORN, HENRY, a hatmaker, married Mary Salton, in Edinburgh on 9 December 1753. [MRE]

DESPRIMMER, ..., a child of James Desprimmer, was buried in Greyfriars burial ground, Edinburgh, on 22 August 1689. [GBR]

DESTINBRUE, WILLIAM, a French teacher in Edinburgh, 1672. [EBR.24.5.1672; 22.11.1672]; married Frances Richardson, in Edinburgh on 23 October 1673. [MRE]

DES VIGNOLES, AUGUSTUS, was admitted as a burgess of St Andrews on 5 October 1756. [StABR]

DEVATIE, THOMAS, a violer in the Canongate, whose testament was confirmed on 7 January 1623 with the Commissariat of Edinburgh. [NAS]

DE VAY, FRANCOIS, husband of Mary Youll, in Dysart, Fife, 1782. [NAS.B21.5.2.423]

DEVEAUX, PETER, was commissioned as a Sub-Lieutenant of the Scots Troop of Life Guards on 25 February 1703. [DAL.V.24]

DEVEREAUX, JAMES, was commissioned an Ensign of the First Battalion of the Royal Regiment of Foot on 1 April 1706. [DAL.V.51/322]

DEVEREAUX, MICHAEL, married Mary Pennock, in the Canongate on 25 December 1792. [MRC]

DE VERGER, ROBERT, valet to Colonel Charles Cadogan, was admitted as a burgess and guilds-brother of Glasgow on 7 May 1716. [GBR]

DE VILLE, ANDRE, born in Anjou, France, settled in Edinburgh in April 1790, residing in St James Square by 1794. [ECA.Aliens Register]

DEVISE, SARA, married Ralph Ralinsone a carver, in Edinburgh on 20 August 1622. [MRE]

DE VO, ANDREW, and his wife Jean Baine, were the parents of James who was baptised in Edinburgh on 1 March 1678. [BRE]; Andrew Dewoe, was buried in Greyfriars burial ground, Edinburgh, on 8 January 1686. [GBR]

DE VO, JAMES, and his wife Jean George, were the parents of Elizabeth who was baptised in Edinburgh on 16 October 1702. [BRE]

DE VOGEL, ANTONY, 1707. [NAS.RD2.94.151]

DE VOUCHT, JAQUELINE, married William Paterson a merchant, in Edinburgh on 21 February 1598. [MRE]

DE VRIGNY, JAMES PHILIP LACOMB, was commissioned Captain of Lord Strathnavar's Regiment of Foot on 18 December 1710. [DAL.V.217]

DIEMAS, PETER, son of the deceased Peter Diemas, was apprenticed to George Drummond a white-ironsmith, in Edinburgh on 30 June 1742. [ERA]

DIEPPE, EUPHEMIA, in Edinburgh, married Robert Morison in Canongate, there on 6 April 1647. [CMR]

DIONISIUS, WILLIAM, a wool-finer, married Bessie Lowristoun, in Edinburgh on 29 January 1633. [MRE]

DIPPIE, WILLIAM, a wright in Leith, 1697, 1705, 1707. [NAS.RD3.87.662; RD2.90.2.571; RD2.94.1030]

DIPPO, JAMES, died 1695 buried in Earlston, Berwickshire

DIPPO, KATHARINE, married Alexander Morrison, in Edinburgh on 19 November 1595. [MRE]

DIPPO, ROBERT, a trunkmaker in Calton, 1665. [NLS#CH.2056]; Robert Dipie, a Frenchman, was buried in Greyfriars burial ground, Edinburgh, on 21 January 1676. [GBR]

DIVO, ANDREW, married Mary Smith, in Edinburgh on 15 October 1663. [MRE]

DIVOGEL, ANTONY, 1707. [NAS.RD2.94.151]

DOE, LOUIS, a merchant in London, 1683. [NAS,RD3.55.554; RD3.56.488]

DOLPHIN, JOHN, was admitted as a burgess and guilds-brother of Edinburgh on 30 July 1755. [EBR]

DONAPIN, JOHN, a shipwrecked Frenchman in Leith, 1658. [ECA.EBR.MB#vii.186.9/3]

DONVILLE, HENRY, and his wife Margaret Bell, were the parents of Henry Bell Donville who was baptised in Canongate on 13 December 1775. [BRC]

DORANDA, ELIZABETH, a spinster in Putney, Surrey, whose testament was confirmed on 1 September 1746 with the Commissary of Edinburgh. [NAS]

DORAT, JANET, married David Mitchell a gardener, in Edinburgh on 15 April 1716. [MRE]

DORAT, JEAN, married Alexander Symson, in Edinburgh on 23 May 1717. [MRE]

DOTCHON, JEANE, married John Smith, in Canongate on 24 January 1672. [MRC]

DOUZET, JEAN, a member of the French church in Edinburgh 1713. [ECA.EBR.17.4.1713]

DOWEN, WILLIAM, a wigmaker in North Kirk parish, married Agnes, daughter of Walter Coutts a smith, in Edinburgh on 11 December 1713. [MRE]

DOWSTINITH, ...,a child of William Dowstinith a Frenchman, was buried in Greyfriars burial ground, Edinburgh, on 13 February 1676. [GBR]

DRAPIER, ABRAM, 1620. [RPCS.XII.355]

D'TASCHER, RENEE, Ensign of the Earl of Portmore's Regiment, whose testament was confirmed on 22 June 1710 with the Commissary of Edinburgh. [NAS]

DU BARTAS, GUILLAUME DE SALUST, a Huguenot poet who visited St Andrews in the 1590s. [PHS#XXVII.698]

DU BERRY, JOHN, master of horse to the Duke of Buccleugh, was admitted as a burgess and guilds-brother of Edinburgh on 16 July 1735. [EBR]

DU BISSON, JOHN, a surgeon who was admitted as a burgess of Edinburgh on 17 October 1799. [EBR]

DU BLAIS, E. M., a French surgeon in the service of the Marquis of Huntly, was admitted as a burgess of Aberdeen on 22 June 1637. [ABR]

DUBLUE, ROBERT, servant to the Provost of Dunbarton, was admitted as a burgess and guilds-brother of Glasgow on 3 September 1700. [GBR]

DU BOURGAY, CHARLES, was commissioned Quarter Master General in Scotland on 11 July 1712. [DAL.V.220]

DU BUISSON, LOUIS, permitted to open a school and teach French and Arithmetic in Edinburgh in 1663. [ECA.EBR:6.11.1663]

DU BURGIE, Colonel CHARLES, was admitted as a burgess and guilds-brother of Glasgow on 3 October 1715. [GBR]

DUCHALL, EUFAME, married John Carrone, in Canongate on 19 December 1615. [MRC]

DU CORNET, JAMES, in Bordeaux, 1641. [NAS.GD18.2408]

DU CORNET, JOHN, eldest son and heir of late James Du Cornet, a merchant in Bordeaux, disposed of rents due from property in Netherbow, Edinburgh, in favour of John Luissignet, merchant in Bordeaux, subscribed there on 17 April 1665. [ECA.EBR.MB#iii/50/2177]

DU FORT, ..., of Captain Robinson's troop in Ayr, 1689. [RPCS.XIV.673]

DU FRERIE, FRANCIS, and his wife Elizabeth Anderson, were the parents of Henry Philip Francis baptised 20 October 1782, Catherine Louisa baptised 17 June 1790, William Adams baptised 10 February 1792, Francis Louis baptised 25 December 1793, and Henrietta Frances Arnold baptised 29 March 1797, all in Edinburgh. [BRE]

DUNBABIN, JOHN, a pin maker in Leith, 1714. [NAS.RD4.114.183]

DUNDELISLE, SIMEON, and his wife Margaret Bowtone, were the parents of Margaret who was baptised in South Leith on 27 January 1656. [SLBR]

DUPASQUIER, LEONARD, a carver and guilder, married Margaret, daughter of John Anderson a smith in Alloa, in Edinburgh on 15 July 1778. [MRE]

DU PASQUIER, MARY, married William Roy a watchmaker, in Edinburgh on 27 April 1787. [MRE]

DU PIN, NICOLAS, subscribed to a contract with the Scots White Paper Manufactury in London during 1694, [NLS#MS1913]; from London to Braid, Edinburgh, by 1695, deputy governor of the paper and linen manufactures of Scotland, England and Ireland, 1697. Founder of the Scots Paper Company in 1694, also of various linen and mining companies in Scotland, plus the White Paper Company of England, and the Irish Paper Company, tacksman of the papermill at Braid 1698. [NAS.RD4.81.735; RD4.80.1203; RD4.82.1744; RD3.89.115; RD4.83.126; RD3.79.109]; was admitted as a burgess and guilds-brother of Ayr on 13 September 1695. [AyrBR]

DU PLISIS, CHARLES, quartermaster of Major General Lanier's Regiment of Horse, in Irvine, 1689. [RPCS.XIV.721]

DU PONT, FRANCIS LOUMEAU, minister of the Huguenot church in Edinburgh 1682-, [PHS.XXII.281;PHS.XLII.xvii]; 1685, [RPCS.XI.303];was naturalised in Scotland in 1707. [APS.XI.484]; Discharge of stipend 1707, 1708, [ECA.EBR.MB#182/ii.18/24]; French minister in Edinburgh 1713. [ECA.EBR,17.4.1713]; in Edinburgh, 1715, [NAS.GD220.5.562; GD220.6.1769.29]; whose testament was confirmed on 11 January 1727 with the Commissariat of Edinburgh. [NAS]

DU PONT, FRANCIS, executor for Captain Peter Cheranton, 1714. [NAS.RD3.141.25]

DU PONT, PETER LOUMEAU, son of the French minister in Edinburgh, 18 August 1731; minister of the French congregation in Edinburgh, 1773. [ECA.EBR.53.452; 90.106; 92.58; 94.325]

DU PONT, SIMON, [1699-1786]; grandson of Francis L. Du Pont, minister of the Huguenot Church in Edinburgh, died March 1786. [PHS.22.281]

DU PONT, ..., was commissioned a surgeon of Lord Strathnavar's Regimen tof Foot on 18 September 1694. [DAL.III.381]

DU PONT, ..., Lieutenant of Colonel Cunningham's Regiment, 1691. [RPCS.XVI.75]

DU POQUE, ..., one of the ministers of the French church in Edinburgh was admitted as a burgess and guilds-brother of Edinburgh on 9 September 1696. [EBR]

DU PRIE, GEORGE, a page to the Duke of Hamilton, was admitted as a burgess and guilds-brother of Glasgow on 15 September 1721. [GBR]

DURAN, ADRIEL, piper of the 1st Battalion of the Royal Regiment of Foot in 1705. [DAL.V.34]

DURANT, WILLIAM, a minister, was admitted as a burgess and guilds-brother of Glasgow on 28 September 1652. [GBR]

DUROURE, Major SCIPIO, was admitted as a burgess and guilds-brother of Glasgow on 26 September 1728. [GBR]

DURY, THEODORE, a French refugee, a Lieutenant in 1689 later Captain, an artilleryman at the Siege of Edinburgh Castle and Blair Atholl Castle in 1689, [RPCS.XIV.xvi/84/421]; married Mary Ann Bourlier, and were parents of Olympia baptised 29 June 1701 in Edinburgh, [BRe]; was commissioned Her Majesty's Chief Engineer in Scotland on 25 August 1702, [DAL.V.226]; and was naturalised in Scotland in 1707. [APS.XI.484]

DU SHANE, JOHN, married Mary Wilson in Edinburgh on 25 February 1686. [MRE]

DU TAILLES, PETER, a staymaker, contracted to marry Janet Muir a widow on 8 November 1793 but the marriage did not occur, but on 25 January 1794 he married Isabella, daughter of William Hanniker a staymaker, in Edinburgh on 25 January 1794. [MRE]

DU TENT, HENRY, was admitted as a burgess and guilds-brother of Glasgow on 8 May 1701. [GBR]

DU VAL, ALEXANDER, a merchant who was admitted as a burgess of Edinburgh on 28 June 1781. [EBR]; he married

Margaret, daughter of William Ferguson a writer, in Edinburgh on 3 July 1774. [MRE]

DU VAL, CLAUDE, servant to the Duke of Lennox, was admitted as a burgess and guilds-brother of Edinburgh on 20 August 1662. [EBR]

DUVANT, JAMES, a minister, was admitted as a burgess of Old Aberdeen on 8 September 1652. [OABR]

EDINGER, ROBERT, a wigmaker burgess in South Kirk parish, married Agnes, daughter of James Pennicook a writer, in Edinburgh on 19 April 1716. [MRE]

EHO, ..., child of John Eho, was buried in Greyfriars burial ground, Edinburgh on 11 June 1672. [Greyfriars Burial Register]

ELIP, EPHRAIM, a soldier in Kirkcudbright, 1689. [RPCS.XIV.758]

ELLIO, ..., a Frenchman in Captain Bassett's troop of General Lanier's Regiment of Horse, in Irvine 1689. [RPCS.XIV.721]

ENZIER, JOSEPH, a plasterer in Edinburgh, whose testament was confirmed on 30 April 1745 with the Commissary of Edinburgh. [NAS]

ESBIE, BARBARA, married John Corsar a weaver, in Edinburgh on 27 December 1696. [MRE]

ETHEW, ELIZABETH, married John Meldrum, in Edinburgh on 5 June1662. [MRE]

ETHEW, JOHN, a perfumer, married Helen Hutchison, in Edinburgh on 5 June 1662. [MRE]

ETTINGER, ANDREW, married Jean Murray, in Edinburgh on 24 August 1686. [MRE]; town officer, was admitted as a burgess of Edinburgh by right of his father Conrad Ettinger a jeweller burgess, on 12 February 1701. [EBR]

EVENCE, HENRY, a mariner, married Elizabeth Hog, in Edinburgh on 13 March 1655. [MRE]

EVVY, DAVID, a gardener, married Marjorie Geddes, in Canongate on 29 May 1694. [MRC]

FALCONER, PHILIP, trumpeter of Sir John Lanier's Regiment in Ayr, 1689. [RPCS.xiv.674]

FASHIER, ..., Captain Lieutenant in Colonel Hepburn's regiment, was naturalised in Scotland in 1707. [APS.XI.485]

FAULCON, ELIZABETH, widow of John Rodolph Tarin minister of the French congregation in Edinburgh, whose testament was confirmed on 27 January 1744 with the Commissary of Edinburgh. [NAS]

FERRE, ANDREW, confectioner, was naturalised in Scotland in 1707. [APS.XI.484]

FILION, PETER, a French Protestant, applied to the Earl of Leven for a post in the army in Scotland, 1708. [NAS.GD26.9.419]; his child was buried in Greyfriars, Edinburgh, on 25 May 1700. [Greyfriars Burial Register]

FLEMING, ANNE, a French spinner in Edinburgh 1733. [ECA.EBR.MB#vii.248.7672/7688]

FLEMING, MARY, wife of James Charlet, daughter of Anne Dassauville, from Picardy via Tournai, and Rotterdam to Scotland, landed at Leith on 10 October 1729, mother of George Augustus Charlet born 11 October 1729. [PHS.XXVII.100]

FOCHON, PETER, in Canongate, married Margaret Straiton from Edinburgh, in Edinburgh on 14 July 1670. [MRC]

FONCONET, EDWARD, a dancing and fencing master in Edinburgh, during the 1660s. [ECA.EBR: 23.11.1666; 17.1.1668]

FONTAINE, ANTONY, a tailor who was admitted as a burgess of Edinburgh by right of his wife Sarah, daughter of John Boyle a vintner burgess, on 30 January 1807. [EBR]

FONTEIN, GILLEAUM, gentleman to the Master of Ross, was admitted as a burgess and guilds-brother of Glasgow on 31 August 1676. [GBR]

FOUCANAL, MARGARET, married James Maxwell a merchant, in Edinburgh on 17 July 1644. [MRE]

FOUNTAINE, EDWARD, master of the revels, 1688. [RPCS.XIII.xliii]; two of his children were buried, one in 1674, and another in 1675, while he was buried on 27 November 1695, all in Greyfriars, Edinburgh. [Greyfriars Burial Register]

FOUNTAINE, JAMES, master of the revels, 1688. [RPCS.XIII.xliii]

FOUNTAINE, MARY, married James Elleis of Huntleywood, in Edinburgh on 30 April 1686. [MRE]

FOUNTAINE, RACHAEL, widow of John Lefevre a French minister in Edinburgh, 1712, [ECA.EBR, 13.6.1712]

FOURCADE, FLORENT, surgeon to the Duke of Buccleugh, was admitted as a burgess and guilds-brother of Edinburgh on 2 July 1679. [EBR]

FOURMONT, CLAUD, master cook to the Duke of Albany and York, was admitted as a burgess and guilds-brother of Edinburgh on 26 December 1679. [EBR]

FOURNIER, JOHN, a Cornet of the Royal Regiment of Dragoons, whose testament was confirmed on 13 May 1707 with the Commissariat of Edinburgh. [NAS]

FOURNIER, JOHN, Cornet of the Royal Regiment of Dragoons, whose testament was confirmed on 13 May 1707 with the Commissary of Edinburgh. [NAS]; his child was buried in Greyfriars, Edinburgh, on 2 April 1693. [Greyfriars Burial Register]

FOYSES, JACQUES, servant to the Duke of Lennox, was admitted as a burgess and guilds-brother of Edinburgh on 20 August 1662. [EBR]

FRAIGNEW, JOHN, a confectioner, was admitted as a burgess and guilds-brother of Edinburgh on 28 September 1705. [EBR]

FRENCH, JAMES, a Frenchman, was buried in Greyfriars, Edinburgh, on 26 August 1675. [Greyfriars Burial Register]

FRENCHMAN, ..., a child of John Frenchman, a Frenchman, was buried in Greyfriars, Edinburgh, on 6 March 1665. [Greyfriars burial Register]

FRONTIN, BERNARD, confectioner to the Duke of Buccleugh, was admitted as a burgess and guilds-brother of Edinburgh on 2 July 1679. [EBR]

FUGARD, JOHN, apprenticed to Paul Roumieu junior in Edinburgh...........................[ERA]

FUNELL, NICOLAS, married Margaret Ferguson, in Edinburgh on 15 July 1662. [MRE]

FUNELL, NICOLAS, married Sarah McClirie, in Edinburgh on 14 October 1683. [MRE]

FUNTANET, NICOLAS, a Frenchman and a clock-maker, was admitted as a burgess of Edinburgh on 2 October 1611 by right of his wife Elizabeth, daughter of John Robertson a maltman burgess. [EBR]

GABELL, CHARLES, soldier of Captain Mordaunt's Company in Ayr, 1689. [RPCS.XIV.674]

GAILLAIS, BOWMAN, 'a Frenchman' in Major General Lanier's Regiment of Horse in Irvine, 1689. [RPCS.XIV.723]

GALANTRIE, LAURENCE, a merchant in Edinburgh, buried 29 June 1700, husband of (1) Elizabeth Cunningham, buried 8 January 1687, (2) Mary Mathie, buried 20 April 1693, parents of children buried 1692, and 1693, in Greyfriars, Edinburgh. [Greyfriars Burial Register]

GALLOW, FRANCIS, a merchant, married Jean Hamilton, in Edinburgh on 21 March 1645. [MRE]

GALZEART, FRANCIS, a resident of Edinburgh, formerly in Montalban, dead by 1660, husband of Margaret Syme. [NAS.GD18.2279]; their child was buried in Greyfriars, Edinburgh, on 2 October 1665. [Greyfriars Burial Register]

GANIE, JANE, (sic), a tailor, his child was buried in Greyfriars, Edinburgh, on 9 July 1660. [Greyfriars Burial Register]

GANUERS, CHARLES, gentleman of Major General Lanier's Regiment of Horse, in Irvine, 1689. [RPCS.XIV.722]

GANWARD, FRANCIS, his widow Margaret Sim was buried in Greyfriars, Edinburgh, on 18 May 1686. [Greyfriars Burial Register]

GARRO, PETER, son of Luke Garro a weaver in Spitalfields, London, employed as a boy interpreter with the French weavers in Edinburgh during 1730s, then apprenticed to John Dallet in Edinburgh. [OEC.XXV.14][PHS.XXVII.104]

GASCOIGNE, FRANCIS, a sailor aboard the St Andrew, whose testament was confirmed on 8 December 1707 with the Commissary of Edinburgh. [NAS]

GASCOIGNE, JAMES, a gunsmith from France, was admitted, on the recommendation of M. La Fevre the French minister, as a burgess of the Canongate on 28 September 1695. [CBR]

GASCOIGNE, JOHN, was admitted as a burgess and guilds-brother of Edinburgh on 18 August 1736. [EBR]

GASCOIGNE, PRIMROSE, married John Welsh a Writer to the Signet, in Edinburgh on 19 April 1772. [MRE]

GASCOIGNE, WILLIAM, a gentleman's servant, married Helen Young from Leven, in Edinburgh on 17 November 1788. [MRE]

GASCOIGNE, WOODRUFF, whose testament was confirmed on 27 May 1775 with the Commissary of Edinburgh. [NAS]

GAUTIER, PETER, a feltmaker, married Jean Thomson, in Edinburgh on 23 May 1694. [MRE]; was admitted as a burgess of Edinburgh on 5 September 1694 by right of his wife Jean, daughter of William Thomson a feltmaker burgess. [EBR]

GEDDIE, ELIZABETH, widow of Peter Petite a sailmaker in Leith, 1715. [NAS.RD4.116.313, 700]

GEINS, DANIEL, Lieutenant of the Earl of Angus's Regiment of Foot, whose testament was confirmed on 5 March 1709 with the Commissary of Edinburgh. [NAS]

GELLIE, ALBERT, a French founder in Old Aberdeen, was admitted as a burgess there on 8 October 1701. [OABR]

GELLYOUR, ROBERT, his widow Agnes Ochiltree was buried in Greyfriars, Edinburgh, on 25 April 1661. [Greyfriars Burial Register]

GENDRON, SYMPHORIAN, servant to the Duke of Lennox, was admitted as a burgess and guilds-brother of Edinburgh on 20 August 1662. [EBR]

GENEST, ELIZABETH, widow of John Samuel Longuet merchant of London, whose testament was confirmed on 28 June 1782 with the Commissariat of Edinburgh. [NAS]

GERAUD, BENJAMINE, a student of medicine, married Susanna, daughter of James Whitelaw a farmer in Jedburgh, in Canongate on 26 August 1794. [MRC]

GIGNOUS, JOHN, a Captain of Buchan's Regiment of Foot in 1696. [DAL.IV.146]

GILLET, NATHANIEL, a goldsmith in Aberdeen, 17........

GILLOT, ELIAS, 1697. [NAS.RD4.81.556]

GINLIS, ..., a French child, was buried in Greyfriars, Edinburgh, on 3 July 1668. [Greyfriars Burial Register]

GLANEDONES, PATRICK, a Frenchman, was buried in Greyfriars, Edinburgh, on 2 December 1675. [Greyfriars Burial Register]

GOBRON, FRANCIS, was admitted as a burgess and guilds-brother of Edinburgh on 9 October 1696, [EBR]; a late servitor to the Earl of Crawford, was naturalised in Scotland in 1707. [APS.XI.484]

GODFREY, JOHN, preacher of the Gospel, was naturalised in Scotland in 1707. [APS.XI.484]

GODINIUS, NICOLAS, born during 1634, son of Nicolas Godinius, a merchant in Havre du Grace, and his wife Judith Duefur, died in Dundee on 4 February 1648. [Howff gravestone, Dundee]

GOOL, DAVID, member of the French church in Edinburgh 1713. [EBR,17.4.1713]

GOUPIL, GILES, a periwig maker from Caen, a member of the Threadneedle Street congregation in London, bound for Scotland in September 1681. [HSQS.XLIX.102]

GRANDPRE, JEAN, member of the French church in Edinburgh 1713. [EBR,17.4.1713]

GRAVENBROEK, JACOB, a Dutch reed maker in Edinburgh, husband of ..... D'Assauville, by 1762. [OEC.XXV.13]

GREBAN, ESTHER, a Frenchwoman, was buried in Greyfriars, Edinburgh, on 14 June 1691. [Greyfriars Burial Register]

GRISSAN, JEAN, married Thomas Johnston, in Canongate on 7 March 1717. [MRC]

GROLEUX, MARTHA, married William Ker a student, in Edinburgh on 14 February 1726, [MRE]

GUERIN, Captain, was admitted as a burgess and guilds-brother of Edinburgh on 7 March 1714. [EBR]

GUERINE, ..., of Sir John Lanier's Regiment in Ayr, 1689. [RPCS.XIV.673]

GUEYELLEM, ..., Major of Colonel Cunningham's Regiment, 1691. [RPCS.XVI.75]

GUIDET, BALTHAZAR, was commissioned as Captain of Lieutenant Colonel Forbes troop in Brigadier Richard Cunningham's Regiment of Scots Dragoons on 1 October 1696; a Major of the Marquis of Lothian's Regiment of Dragoons at Queensferry on 22 September 1703, [DAL.V.207]; Major of Colonel William Kerr's Regiment of Dragoons [7th Hussars], 1713. [DAL.IV.120; V.210]

GUILLEAUME, PETER, born in 1802, died 27 August 1831; Helen Marriet Guilleaume, died 5 July 1842; son Clement Villeneuve died on 30 May 1824, aged 6 weeks, and son Henry Peter died on 14 January 1827, aged 1.5 years. [Montrose, Angus, g/s]

GUILLEMOT, PETER, a French watchmaker, admitted as a burgess and guilds-brother of Edinburgh on 29 August 1688. [E BR]

GUILLIAM, JACQUES, a Frenchman, was admitted as a burgess of Edinburgh on 30 June 1568. [EBR]

GUYDETT, Major BELTHAZER, Captain of Dragoons in Lord Lothian's Regiment, was naturalised in Scotland in 1707. [APS.XI.484]

GWSYWNG, ..., child of James Gwsyng, a Frenchman, was buried in Greyfriars, Edinburgh, on 15 August 1699. [Greyfriars Burial Register]

HAIVIE, JOHN, son of John Haivie, silk-weaver in South West parish, married Christian, daughter of Thomas Grieve a farmer in Dunbar, in Edinburgh on 4 April 1721. [MRE]

HATENVAL, JAMES, a poor Frenchman, was buried in Greyfriars, Edinburgh, on 13 May 1697. [Greyfriars Burial Register]

HAUTYER, PIERRE, 31 December 1594. [NAS.RH15.29.50]

HECLEBERK, INGILBERT, a jeweller, was admitted as a burgess of the Canongate on 31 August 1643. [CBR]

HENMAN, CORNELIUS, a weaver from Maeson, Flanders, then in Norwich bound for Scotland in 1601. [EBR.MB#vii.209/7551, 7570]

HEPBURN, CHARLES, a Frenchman, married Margaret Boyd, in Edinburgh on 31 December 1672. [MRE]

HIEBERDIER, Lieutenant, a prisoner in Canongate Tolbooth, 1690. [RPCS.XV.517]

HIEU, JACQUES, a French gilder and japanner in Edinburgh, was licenced to operate within Edinburgh provided that he took on indigeneous apprentices, 1695, [EBR, 28.8.1695]; 1709, [EBR:11.11.1709]; he was admitted as a burgess of Edinburgh in 1711, [EBR]; member of the French church in Edinburgh 1713. [EBR,17.4.1713]

HILL, SCIPIO, Colonel of HM Regiment of Foot Guards, was naturalised in Scotland in 1707. [APS.XI.484]

HOOD, ..., a Frenchman, was buried in Greyfriars, Edinburgh, on 20 February 1699. [Greyfriars Burial Register]

HOOD, ..., child of a Frenchman, was buried in Greyfriars, Edinburgh, on 1 January 1697. [Greyfriars Burial Register]

HOUBLON, JAMES, was admitted as a burgess and guilds-brother of Edinburgh on 3 September 1707. [EBR]

HOUSSET, JACQUES, a weaver who settled in Edinburgh during 1712. [NAS.NG1.1.2]

HOWBOISE, ..., a vintner, Don's Close, Edinburgh, 1752.
[GED.26]

HUE, HENRIETTA, married Jacob Fleming a weaver, in
Edinburgh on 6 March 1748. [MRE]

HUE, HENRY, a gilder, was naturalised in Scotland in 1707.
[APS.XI.484]

HUE, JAMES, a French gilder, was admitted as a burgess of
Edinburgh on 17 January 1711. [EBR]

HUE, MICHAEL, a gilder at Brown's, President's Stairs,
Edinburgh, 1752. [GED.26]

HUE, ...,child of Henry Hue a gilder, was buried in Greyfriars,
Edinburgh, on 9 June 1699. [Greyfriars Burial Register]

HUGUETON JOHN HENRY, a French Protestant, was
naturalised in Scotland in 1707. [APS.XI.484]

HUIKS, MARGARET, married Henry Bruiks a silkweaver, in
Edinburgh on 8 October 1708. [MRE]

HUINAMON, SUSAN, married John Brown a cork cutter, in
Edinburgh on 17 February 1751. [MRE]

IVET, PATRICK, a cooper, married Agnes Brown, in Edinburgh,
on 19 December 1661. [MRE]

IVY, JOHN, a silk weaver, married Jean Murray, in Edinburgh on 5
March 1661. [MRE]

IVY, JOHN, son of John Ivy a silk weaver, was apprenticed to John
McMorland a merchant in Edinburgh on 14 December 1670.
[ERA]; married (1) Giles Samuel, in Edinburgh, on 27
November 1685, (2) Elizabeth Clunie, in Edinburgh, on 12
August 1686; and Agnes Finlawson, daughter of the late John
Finlawson a merchant burgess of Haddington, on 5 January
1700. [MRE]

JACQUES, ROWLAND, land surveyor of the Customs at Bo'ness, whose testament was confirmed on 18 April 1775 with the Commissary of Edinburgh. [NAS]

JAIP, ALEXANDER, a feltmaker, married Agnes Beir, in Edinburgh on 8 September 1672. [MRE]

JAMART, JACOB, a merchant in Bordeaux, was admitted as a burgess and guilds-brother of Ayr on 29 May 1671. [AyrBR]; also of Edinburgh on 14 January 1674. [EBR]

JANNWARY, PETER, a feltmaker, married Margaret Munro, in Canongate on 19 June 1691. [MRC]

JORRAINES, ..., Ensign of Colonel Cunningham's Regiment, 1691. [RPCS.XVI.437]

JORRENS, BENJAMIN, Ensign of Buchan's Regiment of Foot, whose testament was confirmed on 3 October 1710 with the Commissary of Edinburgh. [NAS]

JOSSY, HENRY, & Company, merchants in Bordeaux, 1671. [NAS.RD2.29.249]

JOURNAN, THOMAS, a book-binder, married Margaret Broadfoot, in Edinburgh on 4 July 1634. [MRE]

JOURNAW, THOMAS, a merchant, married Elizabeth Woodhoue, in Edinburgh on 23 August 1614. [MRC]

JOYANG, JOHN, a felt-maker, married Agnes Fender, in Edinburgh on 29 March 1694. [MRE]

JUIET, HENRY, macer to the High Court of Justice, was admitted as a burgess and guilds-brother of Glasgow on 3 May 1656. [GBR]

JUSTIE, LOUIS, a French jeweller and a burgess of the Canongate in 1696. [OEC.19.19]

KEIGO, JAMES, Captain of Row's Regiment of Fusiliers, whose testament was confirmed on 30 January 1710 with the Commissary of Edinburgh. [NAS]

KREMBERG, JAMES, page to my Lord Commissioner, was
naturalised in Scotland in 1707. [APS.XI.484]

KRESSAU, JOHN, was admitted as a burgess and guilds-brother of
Edinburgh on 25 May 1737. [EBR]

LA BARGE, JACQUES, in Leith, husband of Sara Damond,
testament confirmed on 25 March 1623 with the
Commissariat of Edinburgh. [NAS]

LABIBELE, ABEL, a Protestant refugee and merchant from
Mazamet in Languedoc, was admitted as a burgess and guilds-
brother of Edinburgh on 15 February 1688. [EBR]; and was
permitted to open a shop on 15 February 1688.
[ECA.EBR.32.191]

LA CADET, PAUL, married Ann Brown, in Edinburgh on 10
October 1781. [MRE]

LA CHELENE, JANET, married John Thomas Baird, in South
Leith on 17 November 1612. [MRSL]

LA CHERE, MARGARET, married John Jousie, in South Leith on
24 November 1640. [MRSL]

LA CROIX, ..., a French Protestant galarian, 1717.
[NAS.GD135.141.11.1]

LA FAFAGETTE, DANIELL, married Anne McGhie, in
Edinburgh on 15 October 1701, [MRE]; a merchant in
Edinburgh, was naturalised in Scotland in 1707. [APS.XI.484]

LA FEVRE, JOHN, a minister of the French Church in Edinburgh,
was admitted as a burgess and guilds-brother of Edinburgh on
9 September 1696. [EBR]

LA FEVRE, ..., Major of Clayton's Regiment, was admitted as a
burgess of the Canongate in 1718. [CBR]

LA FOUNTANE, CHARLES, a trooper of Hayfoord's Dragoons
at Dumfries 3 October 1689. [RPCS.XIV.685]

LA FOUR, PETER, son of the late Peter La Four servant to the Marquis of Tweeddale, was apprenticed to John Cope a periwig-maker in Edinburgh on 3 August 1698. [ERA]

LA FRIZE, ANNE, married James Agnew a merchant, in Edinburgh on 21 February 1706. [MRE]

LA FRIZE, PATRICK, a merchant was admitted as a burgess and guilds-brother of Edinburgh, having been apprenticed to James Agnew a merchant burgess and guilds-brother, on 13 June 1733. [EBR]

LAINE, JOHN, a cloth worker in London, 1682, [NAS.RD3.53.127]

LALAINE, PATRICK, a factor in Bordeaux, was admitted as a burgess and guilds-brother of Ayr on 25 June 1687. [ABR]

LA MARE, Captain WILLIAM, 1594. [NAS.RH15.29.50]

LA MARR alias BISHOP, PETER, servitor to the Earl of Strathmore, was naturalised in Scotland in 1707. [APS.XI.484]

LE MERCHAND, DAVID, an ivory cutter, was permitted to open a shop in Edinburgh on condition he instructed the children of burgesses, 12 February 1696. [ECA.EBR.35.236]

LAMOR, WILLIAM, son of John Lamor and his wife Lilias Watson, who was baptised in Edinburgh on 20 May 1655. [BRE]

LAMOTE, CHARLOT STUART, married David Wood a sailor, in Edinburgh on 7 April 1765. [MRE]

LAMOTE, MARTHA, married Captain William Smith, in Edinburgh on 13 March 1768. [MRE]

LAMPAIN, GEORGE, a clerk to the stables of the Duke of Albany and York, was admitted as a burgess and guilds-brother of Edinburgh on 26 December 1679. [EBR]

LAMPREUR, STEPHAN, servant to Lord George Gordon, was admitted as a burgess of Aberdeen on 30 August 1631. [ABR]

LAMSBE, PETER, and his wife Adlaid Lamote, were parents of Francise a daughter who was baptised in Edinburgh on 10 June 1726. [BRE]

LAMURE, JANET, married James Berrie a shoemaker, in Edinburgh on 22 November 1723. [MRE]

LANGRANG, DIONISIOUS, servant to the Earl of Denby, was admitted as a burgess of Glasgow on 7 October 1628. [GBR]

LAPINE, NICOLAS JONQUEL, a tailor in the parish of St Paul's, Covent Garden, London, 1702. [NAS.RD2.86.1.152]

LA PONGE, FRANCIS PETER, surgeon to the Duke of Argyll, was admitted as a burgess and guilds-brother of Glasgow on 9 March 1716. [GBR]

LA PONGE, PETER, was commissioned surgeon of the Scots {4ᵗʰ} Troop of Life Guards on 6 March 1708; and on 29 July 1712 he was commissioned surgeon of Edinburgh Castle. [DAL.V.205/220]

LA PONGE, ..., 1700. [NAS.RD4.87.387]

LARINE, JEAN, in Edinburgh, married John Eddie, in Canongate on 19 April 1744. [MRC]

LA ROON, MARCELLUS, a Lieutenant of the First Battalion of the Royal Regiment of Foot in 1709. [DAL.V.322]

LA ROUSE, PETER, and his wife Marion Fairholm, were parents of Peter baptised on 31 March 1635, John baptised on 27 June 1641, and Robert baptised on 14 January 1644, all in Edinburgh. [BRE]

LA SAGETT, DANIEL, a japanner and merchant in Edinburgh, was licensed to operate within Edinburgh, provided that he instructed local children, 1695, [EBR, 28.8.1695]; 1697, 1700, 1702, 1706. [NAS.RD4.80.1203; RD3.94.270-294; RD2.86.1.419; RD2.92.684; GD18/5367]; a merchant burgess, who married Anne, daughter of William McGhie late minister at Aberlady, in Edinburgh on 15 October 1701. [MRE]

LASAVEWER, CHARLOTTE, married William Thomson a drum major, in Edinburgh on 30 August 1800. [MRE]

LATHEIS, LUCRETIA, married Robert Horne, in Edinburgh on 20 December 1610. [MRC]

LATRICK, JOHN, a wright in Portsburgh, testament confirmed on 14 January 1654 with the Commissariat of Edinburgh.???

LAUMAN, HENRY LOUIS, a gentleman's servant, married Mary Reid from Aberdeen, in Edinburgh on 20 December 1800. [MRE]

LAUROON, MARCELLUS, Captain of Stanhope's Regiment of Dragoons, was admitted as a burgess and guilds-brother of Glasgow on 9 January 1716. [GBR]

LAVAUX, MATILDA, daughter of Thomas Lavaux in Edinburgh, married Abraham Moffet, in Canongate on 13 September 1797. [MRC]

LAVAUX, THOMAS, husband of Sophia Boswell, parents of Euphan who was baptised in Edinburgh on 14 August 1773. [BRE]

LAVAVASTER, ESAY, father of Jean or Janet who was baptised in Edinburgh on 18 January 1597. [BRE]

LAVI, HENRY, a factor at Bordeaux, was admitted as a burgess and guilds-brother of Edinburgh on 1 September 1671. [EBR]

LAVIE, HENRY, a sailor from Bordeaux, was admitted as a burgess and guilds-brother of Ayr on 15 August 1760. [AyrBR]

LAVIE, JOHN, son of Hugh Lavie a factor in Bordeaux, was admitted as a burgess and guilds-brother of Ayr on 30 August 1686. [ABR]

LAWRITAN, JOHN, a burgess of Bordeaux, was admitted as a burgess of Aberdeen on 4 May 1665. [ABR]

LE BAS, PAUL, Ensign of the Earl of Portmore's regiment, whose testament was confirmed on 23 November 1710 with the Edinburgh. [NAS]

LE BEAU, JACOB, captain of the frigate Brile, was admitted as a burgess and guilds-brother of Edinburgh on 14 October 1690. [EBR]

LE BLANC, AENEAS, a native of La Rochelle, was naturalised in Scotland, 1707. [APS.XI.485]

LE BLANC, CAJET, valet to General William Cadogan, was admitted as a burgess and guilds-brother of Glasgow on 7 May 1716. [GBR]

LE BLANC, ELIAS, husband of Isobel Campbell, parents of Christian baptised in Edinburgh on 4 November 1686, and of John baptised in Edinburgh on 10 August 1690. [BRE]

LE BLANC, JAMES, a French protestant, was admitted as a burgess and guilds-brother of Edinburgh on 2 December 1698. [EBR]

LE BLANC, JAMES, a Lieutenant of Lord Tullibardine's Regiment, husband of Elizabeth, daughter of John Houston of Wester Southbar, later a merchant in Edinburgh, 1697, 1698, 1699, 1700, 1701, 1705, 1706, 1707, was admitted as a burgess and guilds-brother of Edinburgh on 6 September 1704, [EBR]; a merchant in Edinburgh, who was naturalised in Scotland in 1707. [APS.XI.484]; disposition of property in High Street, Edinburgh, to James le Blanc, merchant burgess, 1712; a merchant in Edinburgh, 1715. [EBR.MB#144/5630] [NAS.RD3.87.612; RD3.87.612; RD2.83.491; RD3.94.294; RD2.85.918; RD2.90.1.264; RD2.91.385; RD4.98.213; RD2.93.95; RD4.100.947; RD4.101.901; RD2.104.452; RD4.117.63]

LE BLANC, Major JAMES, married Agnes Maxwell, daughter of the laird of Middlebie, and widow of William Clerk an advocate, in Edinburgh on 26 July 1725, [MRE]; of Edinburgh Castle, whose testament was confirmed on 22 March 1731 with the Commissariat of Edinburgh. [NAS]

LE BLANC, LEWES, was baptised in Edinburgh on 12 December 1726, son of Lewes Le Blanc and his wife Janet Lauder. [BRE]

LE BLANC, SIMON, a merchant in London, 1698. [NAS.RD2.81.2.407]

LE BLANC, ..., a Lieutenant of Lord Murray's Regiment of Foot in 1694. [DAL.III.386]

LE BLANC, Mme., of the Boarding School in Cant's Close, Edinburgh, 1752. [GED.30]

LE BLANE, ANNA, widow of Dr Alexander Colvill of Kincairn, 1682. [NAS.RD2.59.650]

LE BLANE, or LE BLANGE, ELIAS, servant to John Bruce of Kinross, was admitted as a burgess of the Canongate on 6 October 1691, [CBR]; was admitted as a burgess of Glasgow on 20 May 1702, [GBR]; master of the wine cellar, was admitted as a burgess and guilds-brother of Edinburgh on 28 September 1705. [EBR]; his child was buried on 29 January 1690 in Greyfriars, Edinburgh. [Greyfriars Burial Register]

LE BLANK, CAJET, valet to Colonel Charles Cadogan, was admitted as a burgess and guilds-brother of Glasgow on 7 May 1716. [GBR]

LE BLANT, ..., child of Elias le Blant, an indweller of Edinburgh, buried in Greyfriars, Edinburgh, on 29 January 1690. [Greyfriars]

LE BOULANGER, ARNOUD, 1697. [NAS.RD4.81.87]

LE BOULANGER, ISAAC, 1697. [NAS.RD4.81.87]

LE BOUSEY, PHILIP, a gentleman, husband of Margaret Blair, 1715. [NAS.RD4.116.550]

LE BRUN, JOHN NICOLAS, a teacher of humanity, married Jean Stewart from Glasgow, in Edinburgh on 1 February 1767. [MRE]

LE CONTE, NOEL, an upholsterer, who was admitted as a burgess and guilds-brother of Edinburgh on 7 June 1749 by right of his wife Isobel Houston. [EBR]

LE FAIRT, LOUIS, his child buried in Greyfriars, Edinburgh, on 7 January 1673. [Greyfriars Burial Register]

LE FENURE, ..., servant to Lord Delmeny, was admitted as a burgess and guilds-brother of Glasgow on 1 June 1716. [GBR]

LE FEUBRE, or LEFEBUCE, JAMES, servant of the Earl of Hyndford, was admitted as a burgess and guilds-brother of Glasgow on 4 October 1716, [GBR]; and was admitted as a burgess of Edinburgh on 12 February 1718. [EBR]

LE FEUBRE, JAMES, a merchant, was admitted as a burgess of Edinburgh on 21 July 1736. [EBR]

LE FEUBRE, JOHN, from Stockholm, was admitted as a burgess and guilds-brother of Edinburgh on 30 May 1760. [EBR]

LE FEVRE, JOHN, a French Protestant minister who hoped to become established in Scotland, 1693, [NAS.GD406.1.3882]; minister of the French Church in Edinburgh, died circa 1712. [EBR, 17.4.1713][ECA.41.74]

LE FEVRE, Major of Clyton's Regiment, was admitted as a burgess of the Canongate ca1718. [CBR]

LEFEWER, or SMITH, WINIFRED, widow of Peter Lefewer, was buried in Greyfriars, Edinburgh, on 24 October 1699. [Greyfriars Burial Register]

LE FORT, alias CORUILLE, LODOVICK, a periwig maker in the Canongate, 1680. [NAS.RD4.46.577]

LE FORT, alias CORUILLE, LOUIS, a periwig maker in the Canongate, 1680. [NAS.RD4.47.51]; husband of Catherine Barnwell, parents of Mary baptised 4 April 1673, James baptised 26 February 1677, and Charles baptised 29 May 1683, all in Edinburgh. [BRE]

LE FRIES, JAMES, writer in Edinburgh, his widow Christian Kay's testament was confirmed on 24 February 1764 with the Commissariat of Edinburgh. [NAS.CC8.8.]

LE FRIEZE, JOHN, glazier, Maynes of Cardiners, 1682. [NAS.RD2.57.585]

LE GEAII, JOHN, a French student of philosophy, was admitted as a burgess of Aberdeen on 30 January 1633. [ABR]

LE GENDRE, JULES, born in Chartres, France, on 28 February 1785, a Lieutenant of the French Imperial Guard, then a teacher of modern languages at Dundee Academy, died in Dundee on 1 September 1840; his wife Jane was born in Dunkeld, Perthshire, on 29 July 1780, and died in Glasgow on 23 December 1848; their son William Cleviller Le Gendre died on 20 May 1824 aged six months. [Howff gravestone, Dundee]

LE GODFREY, EDWARD, married Margaret Fraser, in Canongate on 10 August 1777. [MRC]

LE GOUCHE, FRANCISCO, servant of Sir Alexander Gordon of Cluny, in Balcomie, Fife, 1630. [RGS.VIII.1574]

LE GOUX, JOSHUA, servitor to the Earl of Roxburgh, was naturalised in Scotland in 1707. [APS.XI.484]

LE GRAND, ALEXANDER, collector of customs at Leith, was admitted as a burgess of St Andrews on 12 September 1730, [StABR] also as a burgess and guilds-brother of Edinburgh on 8 December 1736. [EBR]; Customs Collector of Leith 1740s. [NAS.RS.Edinburgh, 126/178; 127/170, 132; 133/316, 342] [NLS#3036,ff.166-9]

LE GRAND, EDWARD, of Bonnington, whose testament confirmed on 27 July 1769 with the Commissariat of Edinburgh. [NAS]

LE GRAND, JEAN, married Alexander Ferguson a writer, in Edinburgh on 17 September 1782. [MRE]

LE GRISE, CHARLES, a merchant from Yarmouth, was admitted as a burgess and guilds-brother of Edinburgh on 12 April 1738. [EBR]

LE LERRE, WILLIAM, sacristan of the chapel of the Duke of Albany and York, was admitted as a burgess and guilds-brother of Edinburgh on 26 December 1679. [EBR]

LE MAISTRE, MARIA, married James McCrae, in Edinburgh on 5 June 1782. [MRE]

LE MAITRE, FRANCIS, Lieutenant of the Royal Regiment of Fusiliers, was admitted as a burgess and guilds-brother of Edinburgh on 7 January 1767. [EBR]

LE MANE, ELIZABETH, servant to Euphame Wilson vintner in the Canongate, 1625. [EBR.MB#I.4/134]

LE MAY, THOMAS, married Bessie Scott, in North Leith on 5 February 1636. [MRNL]

LE MORIMER, PIERRE alias PATRICK, was commissioned Ensign of Lord Murray's Regiment of Foot in April 1694; commissioned a Lieutenant on 14 October 1696; commissioned an Ensign of the Royal Scots on 1 July 1702; wounded at Schellenberg; recommended for a Company in the New Levies in 1706 by the Earl of Orkney; an Ensign of the 1st Battalion of the Royal Regiment of Foot by 1705; fought at Blenheim. [DAL.III.386; IV.153; V.33/35]

LE MUET, …., 1698. [NAS.RD2.81.2.407]

LE NAIN, MARTIN NICOLAS, a cook, married Elizabeth Wilson, in Edinburgh on 8 January 1782, [MRE]; a grocer, who was admitted as a burgess of Edinburgh on 21 September 1786. [EBR]

LE NEIRE, …., a Lieutenant of Lord Murray's Regimen tof Foot in 1694. [DAL.III.386]

LE NOIR, alias BLACK, CHRISTOPHER, a muff-maker in the Canongate, 1683. [NAS.RD2.62.556]

LENRIEAUX, ANTHONY, a felt-maker, husband of Marian Middleton, 17...[MRE]

LE PEYNT, NICOLAS, a gentleman yeoman to the Duchess of Albany and York, was admitted as a burgess and guilds-brother of Edinburgh on 26 December 1679. [EBR]

LE PIPER, JACQUES, married Elizabeth Van Naersen, in South Leith on 3 July 1604. [MRSL]; parents of Sophia baptised on 12 April 1607 in South Leith. [BRSL]

LE PONGE, FRANCIS PETER, surgeon to the Duke of Argyll, was admitted as a burgess and guilds-brother of Edinburgh on 24 February 1716. [EBR]; also, as a burgess and guilds-brother of Glasgow on 9 March 1716. [GBR]

LERGE, HENRY, a servant of the Duke of Hamilton, was admitted as a burgess and guilds-brother of Glasgow on 15 September 1721. [GBR]

LERGEAN, PETER, a wigmaker, married Agnes, daughter of William Stewart a wigmaker, in Edinburgh on 21 November 1756. [MRE]

LE ROI, LOUIS, born 1766, former cook to the Count of Montboissier, Lieutenant General of the Armies of the King of France, settled in Edinburgh by 1798. [ECA.Aliens Register]

LEROMONIE, ANTHONY, a gunner, was buried on 5 June 1684, and his child on 17 October 1684, both in Greyfriars, Edinburgh. [Greyfriars Burial Register]

LE ROUGE, JACQUES, a cloth-maker from Maeson, Flanders, then in Norwich to come to Scotland, 1601. [EBR.MB#vii.209/7551]

LE ROYE, CLAUDIA, married John Dassauville, in St Cuthbert's, Edinburgh, on 19 April 1737. [MRStC]

LE SASSIER, PETER, and his wife Christian Smith Hamilton, were the parents of Alexander baptised in Edinburgh on 12 September 1787. [BRE]

LESCONCE, ALEXANDER, a merchant, married Margaret Thomas, in Edinburgh on 29 December 1659. [MRE]

LESSEBURIE, PIERRE, a French servant of the Duke of Lauderdale, was admitted as a burgess and guilds-brother of Edinburgh on 7 January 1674. [EBR]

LESSENCE, ALEXANDER, a merchant in Haddington, husband of Margaret Cockburn, 1631. [NAS.RS.Haddington.17/65-67]

LESSERTEUR, PHILLIP, master cook to the Duchess of Albany and York, was admitted as a burgess and guilds-brother of Edinburgh on 26 December 1679. [EBR]

LE TUSE, PHILIP, governor of Basil Hamilton of Baldoon, was admitted as a burgess and guilds-brother of Glasgow on 25 July 1713. [GBR]

LEUIS, JAMES, was buried in Greyfriars, Edinburgh, on 22 December 1671. [Greyfriars Burial Register]

LEUNIS, GEORGE, his children were buried 1670, 1671, 1672, in Greyfriars, Edinburgh. [Greyfriars Burial Register]

LEUREUX, ANTHONY, a Frenchman and former apprentice to Isaac Falcon a feltmaker burgess, was admitted as a burgess and guilds-brother of Edinburgh on 3 January 1701, [EBR]; also was admitted as a burgess of the Canongate on 17 September 1703, [CBR]; a felt-maker in Edinburgh, 1705. [NAS.RD3.106.388]; hat-maker in Edinburgh, whose testament was confirmed on 25 July 1729 with the Commissariat of Edinburgh. [NAS]

LEUREUX, DAVID, son of John Leureux a cupper in France, was apprenticed to Anthonie Leureux a hat-maker burgess of Edinburgh, there on 15 July 1702, [ERA]; admitted as a burgess of the Canongate as a former apprentice to Anthony Leureux, during Michaelmas 1720. [CBR]

LEVENY, JANET, married James Duff, in the Canongate on 30 July 1616. [MRC]

LEVERANCE, JAMES, a stabler, married Janet Henryson, in Edinburgh on 20 January 1614. [MRE]

LEVERANCE, JANET, married (1) Thomas Lindsay a mason, in Edinburgh on 25 January 1625, and (2) John Henryson, in Edinburgh, on 1 December 1629. [MRE]

L'EVESQUE, FRANCIS OLIVIER, born 1753 in Caen, Normandy, later in Bayeux, Normandy, arrived in Jersey on 4 September 1792, a teacher of French residing at Mrs Barclay's, Calton Hill, Edinburgh, by 1804. [ECA.SL115.2.2/30]

LEWIT, MUSIE, a poor Frenchman, was buried on 5 January 1696 in Greyfriars, Edinburgh. [Greyfriars Burial Register]

LICET, MARGARET, daughter of John Licet in Canongate, married William Smith a soldier of the Angus Volunteers, in Canongate on 25 October 1797. [MRC]

LIGAS, J., surgeon's mate of the First Battalion of the Royal Regiment of Foot at the Battle of Blenheim in 1705. [DAL.V.33]

LISCET, ALEXANDER, a journeyman baker, married Jean, daughter of James Drummond a labourer at Abbeyhill, in Canongate on 30 April 1709. [MRC]

LISLE, PETER, a vintner who was admitted as a burgess and guilds-brother of Edinburgh on 1 July 1730. [EBR]

LISOTT, MARGARET, married John Crosbie a shoemaker, in Canongate on 12 May 1772. [MRC]

LISSIGNET, JOHN, in Bordeaux, 1641. [NAS.GD18.2408]

LODER, BECK, sub-brigadier of a troop of Guards, was admitted as a burgess of Glasgow on 17 November 1705. [GBR]

LONGUET, ANNA MARIA, a spinster of Crosby Square, London, whose testament was confirmed on 11 February 1742 with the Commissary of Edinburgh. [NAS]

LONGUET, JOHN SAMUEL, sometime a merchant in London, then in Devon, whose testament was confirmed on 12 December 1754 with the Commissary of Edinburgh. [NAS]

LONGUEVILLE, Dr THOMAS, a naval surgeon, married Helen Moffat a widow, in Edinburgh on 12 April 1767. [MRE]

LOUMEA DU PONT, FRANCIS, late French minister of the Gospel in Edinburgh, whose testament was confirmed on 11 January 1727 with the Commissary of Edinburgh. [NAS]

LUCAS, GUILLAUME, a periwig maker who arrived in London from Caen in September 1681, bound for Scotland. [HSQS.XLIX.132]

LUSSIGNET, JOHN, a merchant in Bordeaux, was admitted as a burgess and guilds-brother of Edinburgh on 1 February 1654. [EBR]; a merchant in Bordeaux, 1665. [EBR.MB#iii/50/2177, 2482]

LYON, JOHN, a hatmaker in the Canongate, married Elizabeth Fendar, servant to Isaac Falcon a hatmaker there, on 14 April 1696. [MRC]

MAINE, JOHN, a soldier of Sir John Lanier's Regiment in Ayr, 1689. [RPCS.XIV.672]

MAINES, DENIS, subscribed to a contract with the Scots White Paper Writing Paper Company in London during 1694, [NLS.#ms1913]; a partner of the company in 1695. [NAS.RD3, 4.4.1698; RD4.28.8.1697]

MALPISE, ROBERT, a barber, married Margaret Ramsay, in Edinburgh on 10 June 1651. [MRE]

MANIE, ..., wife of Anthony Manie a Frenchman, was buried on 8 November 1687 in Greyfriars, Edinburgh. [Greyfriars Burial Register]

MANLENES, HEZACRIS, goldsmith who was buried on 14 December 1690, Greyfriars, Edinburgh. [Greyfriars Burial Register]

MANSIOUNNE, ANDREW, married Margaret Watson, in the Canongate on 25 April 1625. [MRC]

MARCELES, JANET, married James Adamson a hat-maker, in Edinburgh on 1 May 1628. [MRE]

MARIE, ABRAHAM, son of the deceased Quentin Marie, a silk weaver in Spittalfields, was apprenticed as a weaver in Edinburgh 1730s. [OEC.XXV.14]

MARIMASSANTINIE, PETER, a confectioner, married Janet Gordon, in Edinburgh on 9 August 1666. [MRE]

MARIN, DAVID, in Edinburgh, was apprenticed to Paul Roumieu a watchmaker in Edinburgh on 6 July 1681. [ERA]

MARLEY, JAMES, a Frenchman imprisoned in Edinburgh tollbooth, liberated 1690. [RPCS.XV.291]

MARLYEONE, DAVID, a tailor, married (1) Marjory Robertson, in Edinburgh on 16 March 1615, and (2) Eupham Readie, in Edinburgh on 25 July 1634. [MRE]

MARRIOT, RICHARD, was commissioned a Brigadier and eldest Lieutenant of the Scots {4th} Troop of Life Guards on 30 June 1710. [DAL.V.205]

MARTELL, DAVID, Captain of Dragoons, was admitted as a burgess and guilds-brother of Glasgow on 6 January 1716. [GBR]

MASSON, DANIEL, a merchant in St Martins, France, 1698. [NAS.RD4.82.26]

MASSOUN, DANIEL, son of Daniel Massoun a factor in La Rochelle, was admitted as a burgess and guilds-brother of Ayr on 18 June 1698. [AyrBR]

MATHREU, HUGH, born in France 1638, died at Jock's Lodge, Edinburgh, on 19 April 1744. [SM.VI.198]

MATTHEW, HUGH, member of the French church in Edinburgh 1713. [EBR,17.4.1713]

MEIL, WILLIAM, late merchant in Rouen, in Edinburgh in 1704, 1707. [EBR, 22.9.1704][NAS.RD4.100.1184]

MEILL, JOHN, an engineer, son of James Meill in Dieppe, burgess of Dundee 17 May 1633. [DBR]

MELL, JAMES, a merchant in Rouen, 1686. [RPCS.XII.162]

MELL, PETER, felt-maker c1664

MELOUF, ..., child of Robert Melouf a grouifir, was buried on 6 November 1675 in Greyfriars, Edinburgh. [Greyfriars Burial Register]

MERCHAND, JOHN, a merchant, was admitted as a burgess and freeman of Glasgow on 3 June 1606. [GBR]

MERCIER, ALEXANDRE, a Frenchman resident in the Canongate, was admitted as a burgess and guilds-brother of Edinburgh on 14 September 1687. [EBR]

MERCIERGALT, J., 1697, [NAS.RD4.81.1057]

MERIBALS, ANTHONY, servant to the Earl of Roxburgh, was admitted as a burgess and guilds-brother of Glasgow on 20 October 1653. [GBR]

MERTON, ARAN, a Frenchman, buried 28 July 1697, in east Liberton tomb, Greyfriars churchyard, Edinburgh. [Greyfriars burial register]

MESUARD, ..., servant of Lord Polworth, was admitted as a burgess and guilds-brother of Glasgow on 6 April 1714. [GBR]

MISENOR, Captain ROBERT, commander of the Warwick, was admitted as a burgess and guilds-brother of Edinburgh on 14 September 1744. [EBR]

MITCHELL, WILLIAM, baker burgess of Edinburgh, husband of Barbara Mein, disposed of the fifth storey above his bakehouse to the overseers of the French Protestant church for the use of their poor, after his death, subscribed 1693. [EBR.MB#iv.89.3872]

MONGIN, JAMES, late Lieutenant of the Earl of Portmore's Regiment, whose testament was confirmed on 2 November 1726 with the Commissary of Edinburgh. [NAS]

MONLONG, PAUL, a cook, was admitted as a burgess and guilds-brother of Edinburgh on 28 September 1705. [EBR]

MONTAIGNE, GEORGE, a Doctor of Divinity and Dean of Westminster, was admitted as a burgess and guilds-brother of Edinburgh on 17 July 1617. [EBR]

MONTAIGNE, ISAACK, was admitted as a burgess and guilds-brother of Edinburgh on 17 July 1617. [EBR]

MONTAIN, JOANNES, a sailor aboard the Unicorn, whose testament was confirmed on 9 October 1707 with the Commissary of Edinburgh. [NAS]

MONTIER, DAVID, a merchant, was admitted as a burgess and guilds-brother of Edinburgh on 23 March 1681, [EBR]; a member of the Company of Merchants in Edinburgh, 1687, [RPCS.XIII.135/155]; husband of Marie Rymor, 1707. [NAS.RD2.94.513]

MONTRESOR, JAMES, was commissioned Captain of the Regiment of Scots Fusiliers on 25 February 1702. [DAL.V.81]

MONTSEGNE, PETER, a Frenchman, was admitted as a burgess and guilds-brother of Edinburgh on 23 August 1661. [EBR]

MORDAUNT, CHARLES, a wigmaker, married Ann Borthwick, in Edinburgh on 22 February 1761. [MRE]

MOSES, THOMAS, a smith in Canongate, husband of Marie Jollie, testament confirmed on 20 February 1690 with the Commissariat of Edinburgh. [NAS]

MOULET, JEAN, a cook in the service of James Murray, 1771. [NAS.GD10.915]

MOULMAR, or **MULINAR, JOHN JOSEPH BRUMEAU,** a probationer in Divinity from Franquear in Friesland, was commissioned precentor of the French church in Edinburgh on 13 January 1714. [EBR, 13.1.1714][ECA.EBR.41.565]; a French Protestant refugee in Edinburgh, 1715, probably the second minister of the French Church in Edinburgh. [NAS.GD220.5.521]

MOXGAM, JAMES, Captain in Colonel Hepburn's Regiment, was naturalised in Scotland during 1707. [APS.XI.485]

MOYSANT, STEVEN, a Frenchman, married Janet Moore, in Edinburgh on 15 November 1655. [MRE]; was admitted as a burgess and guilds-brother of Edinburgh on 4 December 1661. [EBR]

MUNZIE, LOUIS, servant to James Marley, a Frenchman who was liberated from Edinburgh Tolbooth in 1690. [RPCS.XV.291]

MURRAY, CHRETIEN, born in the Duchy of Brandenburg, son of William Murray a Scot, an officer of the British Army by 1689. [PHS.XXVII.695]

NAUDEN, ANTHONIE, and his wife, French Protestants in Glasgow around 1685. [GBR:16.5.1685]

NEWHOUSE, DANIEL, a Frenchman and Professor of Navigation in Aberdeen, was admitted as a burgess of Old Aberdeen on 17 October 1695. [OABR]; in Edinburgh around 1693. [ECA.EBR.SL1/1/34/221]

NISBET, ELIAS, born in Mirambeau near Bordeaux, son of George Nisbet a Scottish settler there, a Protestant, was naturalised in Scotland on 20 August 1685. [RPCS.XI.159]

NOEL, BENNET, Colonel of the Guards, was admitted as a burgess and guilds-brother of Edinburgh on 21 September 1743. [EBR]

NOTER, ROBERT, a felt-maker, married Catherine Hodge, in Edinburgh on 26 May 1653. [MRE]

NOTTA, THOMAS, a hat-maker, was admitted as a burgess by right of his wife Catherine, daughter of Thomas Hodge a burgess, on 3 May 1654. [EBR]

NOYER, ISOBEL, married Guy Saunegrain, a Frenchman, in Edinburgh on 15 March 1670. [MRE]

OGRIE, WILLIAM, a merchant, married Sibilla Hodge, in Edinburgh on 6 October 1608. [MRE]

OTTINGAR, CONRAD, a goldsmith in the Canongate, 1648. [OEC.19.14]

PADGETT, JOHN, servant to Major Wightman, was admitted as a burgess and guilds-brother of Glasgow on 27 January 1714. [GBR]

PALLAT, ARNOLD, a merchant in Bordeaux, was admitted as a burgess and guilds-brother of Ayr on 31 July 1686. [AyrBR]

PALLAT, PETER, a merchant in Bordeaux, 16... [NAS.RH15.116.2]

PALLISAIR, Captain, master of the Seahorse who was admitted as a burgess and guilds-brother of Edinburgh on 11 September 1754. [EBR]

PALLISER, HUGH, a gentleman who was admitted as a burgess and guilds-brother of Edinburgh on 6 October 1736. [EBR]

PANNANGOE, HEW, servant to George Maule of Panmure, was admitted as a burgess of Glasgow on 14 July 1645. [GBR]???

PANNANGOE, SIMON, servant to the Earl of Loudoun, was admitted as a burgess of Glasgow on 14 July 1645. [Greyfriars burial register]

PAPILLION, or POMPILLION, DAVID, a native of Paris, granted letters of denization on 3 November 1610. [NAS.GD213.53]

PARENT, LOUIS, a merchant from Rouen, trading in Burntisland, Leith, and in Edinburgh, 1648. [EBR: 10.11.1648]

PASCAL, PETER, buried in Greyfriars churchyard, Edinburgh, on 27 April 1689. [Greyfriars Burial Register]

PASCAL, PETER, late Lieutenant of Sir William Douglas's Regiment, 'a refugee from religious persecution in France', with a wife and three children, was admitted as a burgess and guilds-brother of Edinburgh on 11 March 1698. [EBR]

PATIS, ...,child of Gairiene Patis, was buried on 23 February 1676 in Greyfriars, Edinburgh. [Greyfriars Burial Register]

PAULET, JOHN, servant of Robert, Earl of Nithsdale, was admitted as a burgess and guilds-brother of Edinburgh on 23 April 1662. [EBR]

PAULIN, CLAUDE, established the manufacture of cambric in Edinburgh during 1730

PAULIN, JAMES, was admitted as a burgess and guilds-brother of Edinburgh on 26 December 1679. [EBR]

PEARLO, PETER, footman to the Duchess of Albany and York, was admitted as a burgess and guilds-brother of Edinburgh on 26 December 1679. [EBR]

PEDIBOE, THEOPHILUS, was admitted as a burgess of the Canongate on 20 July 1676 by right of his wife Elizabeth, daughter of Thomas Gray a hammerman. [CBR]; married (1) Elizabeth Gray, in the Canongate on 19 January 1675, [CMR]; married (2) Anna Cochran, in Edinburgh, on 13 November 1679. [MRE]

PEGOU, PAUL, an Ensign of Morrison's Regiment of Foot, was admitted as a burgess and guilds-brother of Glasgow on 9 March 1716. [GBR]

PELLORT, GEORGE, mariner in the Canongate, 1682. [NAS.RD4.51.229]

PEPILY, JOHN, was admitted as a burgess and freeman of Glasgow on 12 May 1609. [GBR]

PERFECT, ADRIAN, a Frenchman, a fringemaker in Edinburgh, was admitted as a burgess and guilds-brother of Edinburgh on 30 November 1687, by right of his wife Marie, daughter of John Scott a merchant burgess and guilds-brother. [EBR]

PERMITTER, ROBERT, a land carriage waiter in Edinburgh, married Marion Robertson, in Edinburgh on 2 August 1752. [MRE]

PEROCHON, JOSEPH ELIAS, a merchant in London, married Agnes Eleanora, daughter of John Dunlop of Dunlop, in Edinburgh on 17 March 1794. [EMR]

PERRIER, GEORGE, a stabler in the Canongate, whose widow, Susanna Taplay, married Wiliam Simpson a hatmaker burgess of the Canongate on 26 January 1704. [MRC]

PESSIER, ANNA, a Frenchman's wife, was buried on 28 December 1697 in Greyfriars, Edinburgh. [Greyfriars Burial Register]

PETIT, CHRISTOPHER, trumpeter of the King's Lifeguard, was permitted to open a shop in Edinburgh on 12 June 1691. [ECA.EBR.33.357]

PETIT, ISAAC FRANCIS, was commissioned as Captain of Colonel John Gibson's Regiment of Foot on 11 November 1695, may have served in Newfoundland in 1697; was appointed Captain-Lieutenant of the Scots Foot Guards on 3 July 1700. [DAL.IV.106/235; V.219]

PETIT, JOSUAH, a litster in Rochelle, eldest son of Josuah Petit a merchant in Rochelle, 1714. [NAS.RD2.103.1.694/5]

PETIT, JOSUAH, a merchant in Rochelle, father of Josuah and Renaud Petit, and elder brother of Peter Petit a sail maker in Leith, 1714. [NAS.RD2.103.1.694]

PETIT, PETER, a French sailmaker, who settled in Leith in 1681, [RPCS.XII.443/444]; married Elizabeth Geddes, in Edinburgh on 5 August 1682, [MRE]; a sailmaker and elder of Lady Yester's kirk, Edinburgh, 1686, [EBR, 15.12.1686]; 1698. [NAS.RD2.81.1.673]; naturalised in Scotland 1707. [APS.Xl.485]; Elizabeth Geddie, widow of Peter Petite a sailmaker in Leith, 1715. [NAS.RD4.116.313/700]

PETITE, General, was admitted as a burgess and guilds-brother of Edinburgh on 24 February 1716. [EBR]

PETREY, JOHN PETER, confectioner to Colonel Charles Cadogan, was admitted as a burgess and guilds-brother of Glasgow on 7 May 1716. [GBR]

PETTY, JAMES, a gentleman's servant, married Margaret Wilson, in Edinburgh on 19 May 1787. [MRE]

PEY, NICOLAS, was admitted as a burgess of Edinburgh on 30 August 1641. [EBR]

PHEASANT, MANSEL, was commissioned Captain of Lord Strathnaver's Regiment of Foot on 9 March 1711. [DAL.V.217]

PHILLIPS, JOHN, a refugee from Francs, 1690. [NAS.GD331.32]

PICHARD, JOHN, a bonnet maker, was admitted as a burgess of Edinburgh on 20 June 1598. [EBR]

PICQ, ..., a dancing master in Edinburgh, 1747. [CM#4227]

PINNOT, LOUIS, Ensign of the Earl of Argyll's Regiment of Foot in 1693. [DAL.III.337]

PIRRABEAU, ALEXANDER, a merchant, was admitted as a burgess and guilds-brother of Edinburgh on 31 July 1700, by right of his father Theophilius Pirrabeau. [EBR]

PIRRABEAU, THEOPHILIUS, servant to the Viscount of Oxford, was admitted as a burgess and guilds-brother of Edinburgh on 4 March 1674. [EBR]

PIRRABEAU, THEOPHILIUS, a periwig maker, was admitted as a burgess and guilds-brother of Edinburgh on 6 March 1678, by right of his wife Elizabeth, daughter of John Gray a merchant burgess and guildsbrother. [EBR]

PIRRAT, JAMES, a tailor who was admitted as a burgess and freeman of Glasgow on 19 March 1584. [GBR]

PISCALL, JAMES, servant to the Duke of Queensberry, was admitted as a burgess of Edinburgh on 6 June 1707. [EBR]

PLAIN, JAMES, a dyer, was admitted as a burgess of Edinburgh on 6 June 1694, by right of his wife Janet, daughter of John Galloway a wright burgess. [EBR]

PLAIN, JANET, married John Craik, both in Tranent, in the Canongate on 19 May 1630. [MRC]

PLAIN, JOHN, hat-maker, son of late Martin Plain a hat-maker burgess, was admitted as a burgess of the Canongate on 4 August 1631. [CBR]

PLAINE, ELIZABETH, in Pencaitland, married John Kemp, in Canongate on 27 July 1656. [MRC]

PLAINE, JAMES, son of Francis Plaine, sometime merchant in Paris who died in Savanna, Georgia, during September 1798, his testament was made up and given up by his sister Rose Marguerite Plaine and his brother John Francis Plaine, his executors, and confirmed on 23 February 1807 with the Commissariot of Edinburgh.[NAS]

PLANT, HENRY, a merchant from London, was admitted as a burgess and guilds-brother of Edinburgh on 5 August 1741. [EBR]

PLANT, STEPHEN, a Frenchman, married (1) Estienette Beauqueine, in Edinburgh on 15 July 1677; (2) a dancing master, married Sybella Gourlay, in Edinburgh, on 21 January 1679. [MRE]

POIZET, Dr ELIAS, a member of a troop of HM Guards, was killed in Leith 1691, brother of the Sieur de la Roche and of George and Isaack Poizet. [RPCS.XVI.213/272/420/548]

POLAIN, ABSALOM, son of Claude Polain, moved from Edinburgh to London in 1757. [PHS.XXVII.107]

POLAIN, CLAUDE, with his wife Catherine Masse, and their children, Margaret and Mary, from St Quentin, Picardy, to London, then by sea to Sunderland and overland to Edinburgh in 1730, settled in Candle-maker Row; he was admitted as a burgess and guilds-brother of Edinburgh on 5 August 1730; a cambric and linen weaver in Picardy, Edinburgh, and master of Alexander Thorburn, Thomas King, James Porteous and William Johnston around 1745, in 1748 he moved to London, where he joined the Threadneedle Street church. [OEC.XXV.8]
[EBR.MB#vi.162/6279][EBR][PHS.XXVII.101/107]

POLLET, PETER, a merchant of Bordeaux, was admitted as a burgess and guilds-brother of Edinburgh on 1 February 1654. [EBR]

PORBIE, JAMES, a hat-maker, was admitted as a burgess of the Canongate on 12 September 1667. [CBR]

PORTEAUX, FRANCES, widow of Patrick Cowan tailor burgess of Edinburgh, whose testament was confirmed on 5 December 1637 with the Commissariat of Edinburgh. [NAS]

POULET, WILLIAM, was commissioned Lieutenant of the 2nd {Scots} Troop of Horse Grenadier Guards on 2 September 1709. [DAL.V.207]

POUTENS, JOHN, a physician, was admitted as a burgess of Aberdeen on 19 September 1633. [ABR]

POYEN, DANIEL, brother of .....Poyen, and uncle of ... Pellet, merchants in Bordeaux, 1715. [NAS.RD3.145.514]

PRATS, JOHN, a barber-wigmaker, was admitted as a burgess and guilds-brother of Edinburgh by right of his father William Prats a vintner burgess and guilds-brother, on 3 July 1717. [EBR]

PRETTY, EDWARD, servant of the Earl of Kinghorn, witness in Glamis, during June 1628. [RGS.VIII.1282]

PRIEUR, NICOLAS, a page to the Duke of Albany and York, was admitted as a burgess and guilds-brother of Edinburgh on 26 December 1679. [EBR]

PROVANCE, JANES, a merchant, was admitted as a burgess and guilds-brother of Edinburgh on 28 September 1698. [EBR]

PROVINCIALL, Sergeant FRANCIS, a prisoner in Edinburgh Tolbooth, 1689, husband of Dorothia. [RPCS. XIII.507/536; XIV.277/583]

PROY, CHARLES, a reed-maker, with his wife Margaret Bochard, and their children John aged 9, Magdalene aged 7, and Charles aged 9 months, from Picardy, via Tournai and Rotterdam to Leith, arrived there on 10 October 1729, settled in Candle-maker Row, Edinburgh; was admitted as a burgess and guilds-brother of Edinburgh on 5 August 1730. [EBR] [PHS.XXVII.101]

PROY, SIMON, a Huguenot in Picardy, Edinburgh, 1799. [PHS.22.281]

PUJOLAS, JOHN, a French Protestant minister and schoolteacher in Glasgow, 1690. [GBR:29.11.1690]

PURVIANCE, JOHN, merchant, husband of Marie Bell, was admitted as a burgess and guilds-brother of Glasgow on 8 February 1649. [GBR]

QUAINTANCE, DANIEL, married Marion Buchanan, in Canongate on 2 July 1749. [MRC]

QUAINTANCE, THOMAS, married Jean Forbes, in North Leith on 11 June 1695. [MRNL]

QUAIS, ROBERT, married Agnes Caiglea, in Canongate on 1 November 1803. [MRC]

QUANTANCE, AGNES, married Alexander Strachan, in Canongate on 10 August 1567. [MRC]

QUANTANCE, CHRISTIAN, married Robert Crawford, in South Leith on 4 May 1616. [MRSL]

QUANTANCE, ELIZABETH, married Mungo Lindsay a cordiner, in Canongate on 14 August 1657. [MRC][MRE]

QUANTANCE, HELEN, married John Young, in Edinburgh on 23 June 1648. [MRE]

QUANTANCE, JAMES, married Helen Dunbar, in South Leith on 25 November 1658. [MRSL]

QUANTANCE, JEAN, married Alexander Baird, in South Leith on 11 November 1617. [MRC]

QUANTANCE, JEAN, married Bessie Jack, in South Leith on 2 February 1649. [MRSL]

QUANTANCE, JOHN, married Agnes Bowman, in South Leith on 8 September 1648. [MRSL]

QUANTANCE, JOHN, married Mary Alexander, in Colinton on 29 December 1659. [MRColinton]

QUANTANCE, THOMAS, married Margaret Carr, in North Leith on 13 December 1692. [MRNL]

QUANTANCE, WILLIAM, married Marion Anderson, in Edinburgh on 6 August 1639. [MRE]

QUANTANES, BESSIE, servant to Thomas Thomson a merchant in Edinburgh, 1694. [EPT]

QUAYNTANCE, JANET, married Nicoll Archibald, in the Canongate on 17 October 1615. [MRC]

QUESNEY, ABRAHAM, elder of the French church in Edinburgh 1713. [ECA.EBR.17.4.1713]

QUESNEY, LOUIS, 1698. [NAS.RD4.83.503]; a stamper, who was admitted as a burgess of the Canongate on 8 March 1701. [CBR]

QUILLEMOT, HENRY, member of the French church in Edinburgh 1713. [ECA.EBR.17.4.1713]

QUINEL, JEAN, a merchant and burgess of Rouen, 1630. [NAS.RH9.5.8.1-6]

QUINTANCE, LAWRIE, a quarrier, was admitted as a burgess and freeman of Glasgow on 21 May 1585. [GBR]

QUINTANCE, ROBERT, a tailor, eldest son of Lawrie Quintance, was admitted as a burgess and freeman of Glasgow on 20 January 1601. [GBR]

QUINTANCE, THOMAS, a tailor, third son of a burgess, was admitted as a burgess and freeman of Glasgow on 1 July 1608. [GBR]

QUINTEIN, HELEN, married Andrew Frissell, in Canongate on 2 July 1605. [MRC]

QUINTEIN, JANET, married John Currie, in Edinburgh on 26 March 1607. [MRE]

QUINTIN, DANIELL, a soldier of Colonel Heyford's regiment in Kirkcudbright, 1689. [RPCS.XIV.753]

RAPHE, BARTILMO, married Maisie Grant, in the Canongate on 22 August 1620. [MRC]

REISAIMA, GASPAR, servant to James, Earl of Findlator, was admitted as a burgess of Edinburgh on 19 June 1724. [EBR]

RENAUD, EDWARD T., born 1806, died in Edinburgh on 20 December 1853, buried in St Cuthbert's churchyard, Edinburgh. [St Cuthbert's g/s]

REVERA, JAMES, married Margaret Penicuik, in the Canongate on 18 December 1627. [MRC]

RINCHE, PETER, a hat-maker, was admitted as a burgess of the Canongate on 27 September 1666. [CBR]

RIVALL, LOUIS, was commissioned Captain of the Regiment of Scots Fusiliers on 25 August 1704. [DAL.V.81]

ROBYNE, ANTHONY, servant to the Laird of Grant, was naturalised in Scotland, 1707. [APS.XI.485]

ROCHE, EUSTACHE, a Flemish miner in Newhaven, 1590. [ECA.EBR:IV.282/534/538]

ROMIEU, PAUL, a watch-maker from France, was admitted as a burgess and guilds-brother of Edinburgh on 6 September 1676, [EBR]; then was admitted as a freeman and clock-maker of the Incorporation of Hammer-men of Edinburgh on 2 June 1677; a watch-maker, 1682, [NAS.RD2.58.219]; a watch-maker and elder of Lady Yester's Kirk, Edinburgh, 1686, [ECA.EBR.15.12.1686]; with a wife and two children in Edinburgh, 1694, [EPT]; died during March 1694 and was buried in Greyfriars, Edinburgh. [Greyfriars burial register]

ROMIEU, PAUL, junior, a watch-maker, was admitted as a burgess and guilds-brother of Edinburgh on 16 August 1682. [EBR];in Edinburgh from 1682 to 1717, admitted as an Edinburgh hammer-man 16 August 1682; naturalised in Scotland 1707; born in France, an eminent clockmaker, in Edinburgh by 1710.[APS.XI.485] [ECA.EBR.5.4.1710]

ROSSIERE, MARK, was admitted as a burgess and guilds-brother of Edinburgh on 12 May 1693. [EBR]

ROSSIGNOTT, FRANCIS, a fencing master, married Katherine Campbell, in Edinburgh on 23 July 1792. [MRE]

ROUILLAC, ALEXANDRE, in Edinburgh, 1794. [ECA.Aliens Register]

ROWAN,...., child of General Rowan a Frenchman, buried 1 April 1665 in Greyfriars, Edinburgh. [Greyfriars Burial Register]

ROYLEY, ANTHONY, footman to Colonel Charles Cadogan, was admitted as a burgess and guilds-brother of Glasgow on 7 May 1716. [GBR]

RUDER, ..., a Frenchman in Captain Bassett's troop of General Lanier's Regiment of Horse, in Irvine 1689. [RPCS.XIV.721]

RUFFIN, LOUIS, a manufacturer, married Mary, daughter of Dr John Steel in Jamaica, in Edinburgh on 16 April 1790. [MRE]

RYNAUT, Ensign PETER, was admitted as a burgess and guilds-brother of Glasgow on 9 March 1716. [GBR]

ST AMAND, PHILLIP, a Captain Lieutenant of Sir Charles Graham's Regiment of Foot in 1694. [DAL.III.396]

ST BONNET, SIMON, a French stocking weaver in Edinburgh, 1709, [ECA.EBR.2.2.1709]; elder of the French church in Edinburgh around 1713. [ECA.EBR,17.4.1713]; a merchant and stocking weaver, who was admitted as a burgess of Edinburgh on 11 November 1713, [EBR]; a framework knitter whose widow Esther Addison married James Wilson a stocking worker, in Edinburgh on 15 December 1734. [MRE]

ST COLAM, ..., child of Peter St Colam a Frenchman, was buried in Greyfriars, Edinburgh, on 3 July 1697. [Greyfriars Burial Register]

ST GEORGE, JOHN, a weaver, married Isabella, daughter of Richard Watkinson, in Canongate on 4 October 1776. [MRC]

ST LEGER, SAMUEL, a Lieutenant of the Earl of Argyll's Regiment, 1695. [NAS.RD3.83.537]; whose testament was confirmed on 9 February 1708 with the Commissary of Edinburgh. [NAS]

ST LEGER, THEODORE, Captain of the Earl of Portmore's Regiment, whose testament was confirmed on 9 February 1710 with the Commissary of Edinburgh. [NAS]

ST LO, Captain GEORGE, was admitted as a burgess and guilds-brother of Edinburgh on 10 May 1682. [EBR]

ST LOMANS, ..., a child, was buried on 23 December 1695 in Greyfriars, Edinburgh. [Greyfriars Burial Register]

ST LOW, Captain, master of the Salisbury, was admitted as a burgess and guilds-brother of Edinburgh on 19 March 1708. [EBR]

ST PAUL, STEPHEN, was commissioned Sub-Lieutenant of the Scots Troop of Life Guards on 9 May 1694. [DAL.V.24]

ST PEIRS, Captain JAMES, quartermaster of Colonel Anthony Heyford's Regiment of Dragoons, in Dumfries, 1689. [RPCS.XIV.676]

SABINE, Major General, was admitted as a burgess and guilds-brother of Edinburgh on 24 February 1716. [EBR]

SALLBLIEAS, Lieutenant, a prisoner in Canongate Tolbooth, 1690. [RPCS.XV.517]

SALOMAN, ANNA, a Frenchwoman who was licensed to sell jewels and precious stones in Edinburgh on 23 June 1669. [ECA.EBR,23.6.1669]

SALOUIR, Lieutenant, a prisoner in Canongate Tolbooth, 1690. [RPCS.XV.517]

SANDRIE, GEORGE, in Edinburgh, married (1) Isobel Porteous, ion Edinburgh on 12 December 1672, (2) Lilias Forbes, in Edinburgh on 29 June 1688. [MRE]

SARRAZIN, DAVID, 1697. [NAS.RD4.80.1203]

SATYRE, ABRAHAM, was commissioned Lieutenant of Major General Maitland's Regiment of Foot at Fort William on 10 April 1712. [DAL.V.212]

SAVARY, JOHN, a causeway layer from France, in South East parish, married Agnes, daughter of John Johnstone a farmer in Kinross, in Edinburgh in December 1723. [MRE]

SAVIGILL, MARY, servant to David Carnegie, was admitted as a burgess of St Andrews on 4 October 1771. [StABR]

SAYER, ELIZABETH, married Thomas Freer a tailor, in Edinburgh on 19 September 1693. [MRE]

SAYER, JACOB, a soap-boiler, married Eupham Billie, in Edinburgh, on 15 March 1678. [MRE]

SCLYRIO, JACQUES, a Frenchman residing in the Canongate, 1633. [EBR, 11.10.1633]

SEMYTOUR, JANET, married John Birrell, in the Canongate on 16 May 1605. [MRC]

SERIANT, WILLIAM, married Agnes Blane, in the West Kirk of Edinburgh on 18 February 1631. [MRC]

SEVANN, EUPHAM, married John Ross a servant, in Edinburgh on 8 June 1714. [MRE]

SEVEYS, JOHN, married Christian Pennycuik, in the Canongate on 8 June 1613. [MRC]

SHAMBOE, JASPER, a Frenchman, married Grizel Row, in Edinburgh, on 16 August 1674, [MRE]; a periwig-maker, a stranger, was admitted as a burgess of the Canongate on 3 August 1676. [CBR]

SHAMBOY, ..., a French minister, was buried in Greyfriars, Edinburgh, on 8 July 1689. [Greyfriars Burial Register]

SHAMMO, FRANCIS, a felt-maker from Noirt in the province of Poitiou, settled in Scotland as a hatmaker by 1686, naturalised as a Scot on 14 September 1686. [RPCS.XII.450/451]

SHAMPNEY, MARION, married Robert McMoran a gardener, in Edinburgh on 7 June 1610. [MRE]

SHEVALIER, JAKLINE, married William Paull a bath-stove keeper, in Edinburgh on 7 May 1669. [MRE]

SHINEBOW, ADAM, a wool-comber in South South East parish, married Mary, daughter of John Phinn a litster in North East parish, in Edinburgh on 23 November 1722. [MRE]

SHOCON, PETER, a Frenchman, married Margaret Straiton, in Edinburgh on 14 July 1670. [MRE]

SIDIE, GASPAR, married Isobel Baird, in Edinburgh on 7 June 1627. [MRE]

SIEN, GOSPER, footman to Colonel Charles Cadogan, was admitted as a burgess and guilds-brother of Glasgow on 7 May 1716. [GBR]

SINEX, ROBERT, a tanner, was buried on 18 June 1658 in Greyfriars, Edinburgh. [Greyfriars Burial Register]

SIRIEN, JOSEPH, a silk weaver who was admitted as a burgess and guilds-brother of Edinburgh on 30 August 1704. [EBR]

SOCHON, ANN, widow of Gilbert Soirs a writer in Edinburgh, whose testament was confirmed on 21 June 1758 with the Commissary of Edinburgh. [NAS]

SOCKETT, JOHN, a wool-comber, married Marjory Johnston, in Edinburgh on 26 December 1682. [MRE]

SOFAGRAN, or NORIE, ISABEL, wife of Gavie Sofagran, was buried on 19 April 1692 in Greyfriars, Edinburgh. [Greyfriars Burial Register]

SOFAGRAN, PATRICK, son of a Frenchman, was buried in Greyfriars, Edinburgh, on 1 April 1675. [Greyfriars Burial Register]

SOJORNER, JOHN, a sawyer, married Marion Forsyth, in Edinburgh on 10 April 1605. [MRE]

SOULLARD, LOUIS, a merchant, was admitted as a burgess and guilds-brother of Edinburgh on 19 February 1690. [EBR]

STAFFNEY, NATHANIEL, was commissioned as Captain Lieutenant of Lord Cardross's Regiment of Dragoons on 18 December 1689. [DAL.III.36]

STALLERS, HENRIE, a pasment weaver resident in Edinburgh, whose testament was confirmed on 3 July 1662 with the Commissary of Edinburgh. [NAS]

STOLENCE, JACOB, a pasment maker, married Bessie Oliphant, in Edinburgh on 2 December 1624. [MRE]

STURMAN, JOHN, a weaver from Maeson, Flanders, then in Norwich, England, to come to Scotland in 1601. [ECA.EBR.MB#vii.209/7551, 7569]

SUEIRAL, JAMES, a Frenchman, who was admitted as a burgess of the Canongate on 26 July 1632. [CBR]

SUEIRAL, PETER, son of Luke Sueiral, was admitted as a burgess of the Canongate on 27 October 1642. [CBR]

SURENNE, GABRIEL, born in Compeigne, France, on 25 October 1777, died 12 September 1858 in Edinburgh, his wife Sophia Le Cointe was born in 1777, and died on 27 December 1866, D. F. Surenne, born 1804, died on 8 May 1861. [Dean gravestone, Edinburgh]

TABET, CHARLES, was admitted as a burgess and guilds-brother of Edinburgh on 25 June 1729. [EBR]

TACCATIS, GEORGE, a saddler, was admitted as a burgess and freeman of Glasgow on 29 April 1589. [GBR]

TALANT, WILLIAM, a silk-weaver, married Jean, daughter of Robert Mitchell a tailor, in Edinburgh on 19 April 1706. [MRE]

TALLIE, JOHN, a cordiner, married Isobel, daughter of the late Andrew Mitchell a tanner burgess, in Edinburgh on 2 June 1699. [MRE]

TALLIE, ROBERT, a cordiner, was admitted as a burgess of
Edinburgh on 2 August 1732 by right of his father John Tallie
a cordiner burgess. [EBR]

TAPLAY, SUSANNA, widow of George Peirier a stabler, married
William Simpson a hat-maker burgess, in Canongate on 26
January 1704. [MRC]

TASSY, JOHN, a maltman, was admitted as a burgess and freeman
of Glasgow on 29 October 1594. [GBR]

TELLY, JAMES, a cordiner, married Margaret Bigholme, in
Edinburgh on 5 July 1667. [MRE]

TESTAS, FRANCIS, was commissioned Sub-Lieutenant of the 2nd
{Scots} Troop of Horse Grenadier Guards on 13 September
1709. [DAL.V.207]

THIBOU, JACQUES, apprenticed to Paul Roumieu junior in
Edinburgh, 1683. [ECA]

TILLY, ALISON, married John Grant, in Edinburgh on 11 August
1700. [MRE]

TINTHOIN, PIERRE, a doctor of Holy Scripture at the Sorbonne,
settled in Edinburgh by 1794. [ECA. Aliens Register]

TITULAR, JOHN, son of John Titular in Corsandan, was
apprenticed to John Mortimer a periwig-maker in Edinburgh
on 9 April 1701. [ERA]

TOBIAS, MARGARET, a servant of William Wilson a merchant
in Edinburgh, 1694. [EPT]

TORIN, ABRAHAM, a hat-maker from Rouen, was naturalised in
Scotland on 16 September 1686; deposed that he was of the
Protestant Reformed religion in October 1686.
[RPCS.XII.470/478]

TOSTIE, LOUIS, a jeweller, married Mary, daughter of the late
John Bissett a merchant in Glasgow, in the French Church in
Edinburgh on 19 April 1696, [MRE]; 1696.
[NAS.RD4.79.985]

TOURS, CLEMENT, a glass-wright burgess of Edinburgh, whose testament was confirmed on 4 February 1631 with the Commissary of Edinburgh. [NAS]

TOURS, CLEMENT, admitted as a burgess of the Canongate by right of his wife Katherine Young daughter of a burgess, on 19 March 1646. [CBR]

TOURS, CLEMENT, a glazier burgess of Edinburgh, whose testament was confirmed on 18 May 1647 with the Commissary of Edinburgh. [NAS]

TOURS, JAMES, a glazier burgess of Edinburgh, whose testament was confirmed on 14 April 1658 with the Commissary of Edinburgh. [NAS]

TOURS, Colonel JOHN, brother of Major Robert Tours of the Scots Regiment of Guards to the King of France, 1666. [NAS.RD2.15.556]

TOYES, JOHN, a weaver, was admitted as a burgess of the Canongate on 17 June 1647. [CBR]

TRANIER, Captain ROBERT, commander of H.M.S. Royal Ann, was admitted as a burgess of Edinburgh on 4 April 1711. [EBR]

TRAPAUD, ALEXANDER, aide de camp to General Husk, was admitted as a burgess and guilds-brother of Edinburgh on 21 January 1747. [EBR]

TREVES, SARAH, daughter of Richard Treves a glassmaker, married Michael Russell a writer in Edinburgh, in Canongate on 6 March 1694. [MRC]

TRUMBET, FABRICK, a soldier of Colonel Langtoun's troop in Kirkcudbright, 1689. [RPCS.XIV.756]

TRUMBET, NICOLAS, a soldier of Colonel Langtoun's troop in Kirkcudbright, 1689. [RPCS.XIV.756]

TURRAM, JOSEPH or RUDOLPH, a French Protestant minister in Edinburgh around 1717; he was authorised to go to England for three months on 19 July 1721. [ECA.EBR.44.101; 48.347/444]

TUSSEIN, ETOALL, an engineer, was admitted as a burgess and guilds-brother of Edinburgh on 12 October 1659. [EBR]

VADARET, PHILIP, cook to the Lord Chancellor, was admitted as a burgess and guilds-brother of Edinburgh on 22 June 1687. [EBR]

VALADGE, GEORGE, married Janet Smart in Musselburgh on 26 October 1690. [MRM]

VALD'GIE, JOHN, a cook, married Janet Mowbray, in Edinburgh on 7 April 1618. [MRE]

VALLETTE, ISAAC, a Huguenot refugee and an apothecary, member of the Threadneedle Street congregation in London, bound for Scotland in May 1682. [HSQS.XLIX.184]

VAN DER BROECK, NICOLAS, from Maeson, Flanders, then in Norwich to come to Scotland, 1601. [ECA.EBR.MB#vii.209/7550]

VAN DER PLANCK, ISAAC, a coach-maker, 1700. [NAS.RD4.86.1188]

VAN HOOGNERF, PETER JOHN, a merchant in La Rochelle who was admitted as a burgess and guilds-brother of Edinburgh, on 29 September 1749. [EBR]

VAN HOUTE, ABIGAIL, a Flemish spinner in Edinburgh, then in Perth, 28 August 1601. [ECA.EBR.MB#vii.209/7571]

VAREILLES, JOHN, was commissioned as an Ensign to Lieutenant Colonel Bowie of Colonel George Hamilton's Regiment of Foot on 1 October 1695. [DAL.IV.104]

VARNAY, THOMAS, a soldier, married Catherine Good, in Edinburgh on 17 September 1657. [MRE]

VARRIE, ROBERT, a writer, married Elizabeth Oswald, in Edinburgh on 25 August 1672. [MRE]

VAUTROLLIER, MANASSES, the younger, a bookbinder, married Elizabeth Meldrum, on 12 August 1621, in the Canongate, [CMR]; 1623. [ECA.EBR.MB#1/4.131]

VAUTROLLIER, MARGARET, married Richard Bartrum, a 'mynder', in Edinburgh on 28 August 1623. [MRE]

VAUTROLLIER, THOMAS, born in Troyes, France, denisized in England in 1562, a printer, a printer in Edinburgh during 1580s, died in London July 1587. [PHS.22.121]

VEILLANT, NICOLAS, servant of the Earl of Kinghorn, married Janet Murray, in Edinburgh on 21 January 1619. [MRE]

VERMONT, PHILIP, from Maeson, Flanders, then in Norwich, England, to come to Scotland, 1601. [EBR.MB#vii.209/7550]

VERRIERE, HENRY, Lieutenant Colonel of HM Regiment of Foot Guards, who was naturalised in Scotland during 1707. [APS.XI.484]

VERT, DAVID, son of the late Patrick Vert in Leith, was apprenticed to James Smart a merchant in Edinburgh on 4 August 1686. [ERA]

VERT, JOHN, a smith in Leith, was admitted as a burgess of Edinburgh on 15 February 1710. [EBR]

VIGNOLES, Major CHARLES, was admitted as a burgess and guilds-brother of Edinburgh on 4 October 1752. [EBR]

VILLETTES, HENRY, was admitted as a burgess of St Andrews on 4 June 1770. [StABR]

VILLETTES, WILLIAM, was admitted as a burgess of St Andrews on 4 June 1770. [StABR]

VILLIERS, Dame ANNA, Dowager Countess of Morton, whose testament was confirmed on 25 January 1655 with the Commissary of Edinburgh. [NAS]

VILLION, JAMES, a sailor aboard HMS Crown, whose testament was confirmed on 21 December 1711 with the Commissary of Edinburgh. [NAS]

VILNEW, ..., footman to General William Cadogan, was admitted as a burgess and guilds-brother of Glasgow on 7 May 1716. [GBR]

VISITELLA, ISAAC, a painter resident in the Canongate, whose testament was confirmed on 9 February 1658 with the Commissary of Edinburgh. [NAS.CC8.8.69; GD18.2499] [PS#100]

VONTRALEUR, ELSPETH, married Richard Smith, in the Canongate on 7 January 1618. [MRC]

WILMOT, JOHN, married Beatrix Cowan, in Canongate on 3 November 1661. [MRC]

WYLEMANT, GEORGE, married Janet Mure, in Canongate on 8 April 1666. [MRC]

WYNDER, JONATHAN, a felt-maker in North East parish, married Marion, daughter of William Potter a wright burgess, in Edinburgh on 25 March 1709. [MRE]

Lightning Source UK Ltd.
Milton Keynes UK
UKOW042056280612

195211UK00011B/46/P